The Uneasy Case for Equalization Payments

The Uneasy Case for Equalization Payments

Dan Usher

The Fraser Institute
Vancouver, British Columbia

Printed in Canada.

Canadian Cataloguing in Publication Data

Usher, Dan, 1934-
The uneasy case for equalization payments

Includes bibliographical references.
ISBN 0-88975-153-6

1. Fiscal Equalization Program (Canada)—Evaluation. 2. Federal-provincial fiscal relations—Canada.* 3. Transfer payments—Canada. 4. Grants-in-aid—Canada. I. Fraser Institute (Vancouver, B.C.) II. Title
HJ795.A1U73 1995   339.5'22   C95-911122-0

Table of Contents

About the author

DAN USHER IS A PROFESSOR of economics at Queen's University in Kingston, Ontario. He is the author of *The Price Mechanism and the Meaning of National Income Statistics* (1969), *The Measurement of Economic Growth* (1980), *The Economic Prerequisite to Democracy* (1981), *The Welfare Economics of Markets, Voting and Predation* (1993) and two volumes of collected papers, *National Accounting and Economic Theory* and *Welfare Economics and Public Finance* (1994).

On the Canadian scene, Usher has been concerned for some time about the reorganization of English Canada in the event of the separation of Quebec. His papers on this theme include "The English Response to the Separation of Quebec," *Canadian Public Policy*, 1978, "How Should the Redistributive Power of the State be Divided between Federal and Provincial Governments?" *Canadian Public Policy*, 1980, "The Design of a Government for an English Canadian Country," in D.D. Purvis ed., *Economic Dimensions of Constitutional Change*, 1991 and "The Interests of English Canada," *Canadian Public Policy*, 1995.

Foreword

THIS IS A VERY IMPORTANT STUDY. It is appearing at a crucial time in the history of Canada and at a turning point in the future of our national fiscal arrangements. It is being published as part of an exploration of the economic and political structure of Canadian Confederation.

Earlier this year in *Thirty Million Musketeers*, a book about the future of our federation, Gordon Gibson pointed out that by the end of this century, the federal government will have lost control over what have been the shared programs of health, education, and welfare. Lacking the budgetary clout to enforce a federal intrusion into an area constitutionally reserved for the provinces, the national government will have to be content with what the provinces individually determine in these areas. Gibson's analysis did not deal with the future of equalization payments, except to remark that there was probably need for change, and that these payments should probably be made to people rather than to governments.

The exact form equalization should take is not specified in the constitution. Its constitutional enshrinement is a reflection of a general consensus that it is something we do in Canada—part of the Canadian fabric as it were. But also, because it "just growed" over a long period of time, and because it is a technical swamp, the equalization payments system has been spared the kind of root and branch dissection that other programs have routinely received. This book remedies that deficiency. Dan Usher has systematically examined the motivations, the methods, and the effects of the current equalization system. He concludes that it should be scrapped or dramatically altered. While I happen to disagree with Usher's proposed replacement and to favour Gibson's approach, The Fraser Institute is pleased to publish this monograph in the hope that it will encourage a detailed and comprehensive reconsideration of this $10 billion dollar program. At the very least, Dan Usher's book must make us all feel very uncomfortable with the economic inefficiency and inequity of the current system and make us want to find an alternative.

Since Usher has worked independently, the views he expresses may not correspond to those of the members or trustees of The Fraser Institute.

—*Michael Walker, Executive Director*
  The Fraser Institute

Introduction[*]

> Parliament and the government of Canada are committed to the principle of making equalization payments to ensure that provincial governments have sufficient revenues to provide reasonably comparable levels of public services at reasonably comparable levels of taxation.
> —*Section 36(2) of the Constitution Act of 1982.*

THIS IS AN ODD AND UNUSUAL CLAUSE for a constitution: more specific than is customary about the instruments of public finance, yet remarkably vague about its ultimate purpose and its intended impact on the lives of Canadians. There is something peculiar about a constitution that does not require redistribution of income among people, that says nothing about welfare, that does not mandate unemployment insurance, though it does allocate jurisdiction, that contains no barrier, other than the very general language about "fundamental justice" in the charter of rights, against people starving to death on our streets, but does nevertheless, in the name of equality, require very specific transfers among provinces through the intermediary of the federal government. One wonders what principle of equality, efficiency, or equity might be at stake?

---

* I am grateful to Scott Daniels and Neil Hepburn for excellent research assistance, to Sam Wilson for comments on the manuscript, to Torben Drews for some shrewd advice, and to Patricia Murphy for cheerfully correcting and recorrecting the manuscript as I changed my mind about the text.

The political rhetoric of equalization is nothing if not dramatic. The place of equalization payments in Canadian society was discussed in the House of Commons on February 8 and 9, 1994 during a debate over Bill C3, a small amendment to the Canadian equalization program. The bill was introduced by Peter Milliken, Parliamentary Secretary to the Leader of the Government in the House of Commons, who referred to "the singular role of equalization in underpinning the unique sense of Canadian sharing" (*House of Commons Debates*, vol. 133, No. 017, 1 Session, 35 Parliament, Feb. 8, 1994, p. 1,036). George Proud, Member of Parliament from Hillsborough, asserted that

> The equalization program marks our compassion as a nation. Because of equalization, no citizen of Canada is a second class citizen, regardless of where he lives. The citizens of Cape Race, Newfoundland, of Montmagny, Quebec, of York, P.E.I., of Watrous, Saskatchewan, and of Vancouver, B.C. are all entitled to roughly the same level of services in government. That is the essence of Canada. That is why this country remains united. (p. 1045)

Not to be outdone in superlatives, John Harvard, Member of Parliament for Winnipeg St. James, said

> the equalization program as we know it embodies some of the great ideals and the great values of Canadians. I cannot think of a much greater ideal under our democracy than sharing one's wealth, sharing one's resources. It is an ideal and a value that all of us cherish. It recognizes that there are those provinces and those people who have it a little better than others. (p. 1116)

Sharing through the intermediary of the government is usually thought to be costly in the sense that you cannot get a dollar's worth of benefit to the poor without causing something more than a dollar's worth of harm to the rich. A transfer of money through the public sector involves administrative cost to the government and an additional cost to the public from the distortion in production as people rearrange their affairs to maximize their entitlements to transfers and minimize their tax bill. That is commonly understood, and is accepted, within limits, as a fair price to pay to assist the poor. Equalization payments are claimed to be different. A few days after the debate in Parliament, Mr.

Guillaume Bissonnette, Director of the Federal Provincial Relations Division of the Department of Finance, informed the House of Commons Committee on Finance that

> One of the most intriguing things about equalization is that from an economist's point of view, there is not just an equity case for equalization, but in fact an economic efficiency argument for equalization. The economic efficiency argument for equalization is that if it's properly calibrated, it prevents people from moving for the wrong reasons. That's the key thing. In other words, in a world without equalization, where standards of services in schools and hospitals were enormously different from province to province, you would see people moving simply to avail themselves of better publicly-provided services, not necessarily because they could get better-paying and more meaningful jobs.
>
> Economic theory tells us that that's what you want. You want people to move for the right reasons, the right reasons being moving from a low-paying job to a high-paying job. They shouldn't move simply because they get better services. (House of Commons Committee on Finance February 17, 1994, p. 1555)

Together, these quotations raise a number of important questions: What exactly is the meaning of sharing in this context? Do equalization payments narrow the distribution of income in Canada, systematically transferring income from all rich people to all poor people? The program is in the first instance a transfer of income from the federal government to the "have not" provinces. Is it in the end a transfer from rich people in rich provinces to poor people in poor provinces, as one might hope, and as the wording of Section 36(2) might lead one to expect? Or is it ultimately a transfer from rich people in rich provinces to rich people in poor provinces, or from poor people in rich provinces to poor people in poor provinces, or even from poor people in rich provinces to rich people in poor provinces? Is the determination of the beneficiaries of the Canadian equalization program random, frivolous, or politically determined? Can we be quite sure that equalization payments are equalizing among people at all?

Does the Canadian program of equalization payments enhance the productivity of the Canadian economy? Is the Canadian national income larger as a consequence of the program than it would otherwise be? Are workers and other factors of production induced to migrate from places where their productivity is relatively low to other places where their productivity is relatively high, or are people induced to remain in poor and unproductive regions of the country when they might otherwise be inclined to go elsewhere? All taxation entails an "excess burden" over and above the payment by taxpayers to finance public expenditure, a social cost as taxpayers divert effort from more productive but more taxed activities to less productive but less taxed activities. Does a program of equalization payments reduce the entire excess burden of public expenditure in Canada as a whole, or is that burden magnified by the program? What are the incentives on provincial governments? Are provincial governments induced to act in ways that are beneficial for the great majority of Canadians, or are opportunities created for provincial governments to increase their entitlements to equalization payments by tax or expenditure policies that are not beneficial for the country as a whole?

Are efficiency and equality—the maximization of the national income and the narrowing of the distribution of income among people—the only relevant considerations in evaluating the Canadian program of equalization payments, or is there more to equalization than that? The progressive income tax has a far larger impact than equalization payments on the dispersion of incomes in Canada, but I doubt whether Members of Parliament could bring themselves to describe the progressivity of the income tax as the "essence of Canada," as one of the "great ideals of Canadians," as expressing our "compassion as a nation" or as the reason "why this country remains united." Can one not see between the lines of these quotations a conviction that equalization payments are right, just, fair, and equitable in themselves, almost regardless of the effects of the program on the size and distribution of the national income? Is the principle that revenues per head among the provinces be the same as long as tax rates are the same really worthy of such a high degree of respect?

These three blocks of questions are the basis for the examination of equalization payments in this study; the program will be assessed under the headings of equality, efficiency, and equity. A program or policy is said to be equalizing if it tends to close the gap between the rich and the poor, narrowing the distribution of income in the country as a whole. A program or policy is said to be efficient if it fosters prosperity in the country as a whole, where prosperity may, broadly speaking, be measured by the national income. Analysis of public policy under the headings of equality and efficiency is commonplace, and I follow well-worn grooves in the use of these categories. Equity is a more elusive concept and my usage of the term here is somewhat idiosyncratic, though not inconsistent, in my judgment, with the special virtue that Members of Parliament and others claim to see in equalization payments. Equity in this sense is an adherence to the customs of society. Rules of equity enable society to assign goods to people peacefully. Property rights are equitable in this sense. It is equitable that a person's property should be returned to him if it has been taken improperly, regardless of whether that person is rich or poor. The tax system is commonly said to be horizontally equitable when people with equal pre-tax incomes are taxed equally and when the tax system preserves the ordering of people on the scale of rich and poor. Equalization payments are equitable in this sense if they remove more conflict among the regions of Canada than they engender.

My assessment of the Canadian equalization program is that the large claims in the quotations at the beginning of this book are almost entirely false. The weight of evidence is that the program does *not* do what it is alleged to do: I cannot show conclusively that the program makes the Canadian distribution of income less equal, or that the national income is reduced, or that Canadian society is less equitable on account of the equalization program. What I can show is that the effects are mixed, that there are opposing tendencies and that commonly-asserted propositions about the virtues of equalization payments are unproven.

One might suppose that a program called "equalization payments" would have to be equalizing on balance, but that turns out not to be so. The equalization program is, in the first instance, a transfer between governments. The ultimate benefit to the poor may be negligible, even non-existent, and it is certainly less than if the federal resources in the program were provided to the poor directly. Nor does the weight of evidence and analysis show equalization payments to be efficient. The program has several effects on the national income, some positive, others negative. One simply does not know where the balance lies. The induced migration may or may not be efficient, depending to a large extent on what other programs are in force. A case can be made that uniform tax rates across provinces are efficiency-promoting, but the incentives on the provinces to adjust tax rates to augment entitlement to equalization payments is almost certainly in the opposite direction. The equity argument also disintegrates on close inspection. The analogy between equalization payments and horizontal equity in taxation is dubious at best. Negotiation among the provinces and the federal government over the detail of the equalization forumula could degenerate into a scramble for funds guided by no principle of equity as the term is commonly understood.

It is remarkable that a program with such wide-spread support among Canadians is so uncertain in its effects and has so little to be said for it. My assessment of the Canadian program of equalization payments is that it has been a mistake, and that the design of the program should be changed radically if the program is to be preserved at all.

Equalization payments are highly complex. The equalization formula is straightforward enough, but the effect of equalization payments upon the economy can be equalizing or disequalizing, efficient or inefficient, equitable or inequitable, depending on detailed provisions in the tax codes of the provinces and the federal government and on the response of taxpayers to changes in tax rates. To sort this out, I try to isolate particular effects of the program by numerical examples, in the hope that the juxtaposition of examples will give the reader a sense of the full impact of the program. Inevitably, this procedure is less conclusive than one would like, but the procedure can be informative against a background where it is often supposed on the strength of a restrictive model of federal-provincial relations that the effects of equalization payments are clear-cut and predictable. The method has the additional advantage that it is accessible to readers not well schooled in formal economics.

Equalization payments cannot be evaluated in isolation. Some public sector programs can be assessed by a simple comparison of the economy with or without the program in question. Equalization payments are less readily analyzed because they are part of a complex machinery of federal-provincial relations. Substantial modification of the equalization program would call for modifications in other aspects of society, especially the division of powers between the federal and provincial governments. The machinery can be altered, but not necessarily one piece at a time. Furthermore, when there is a significance chance that Quebec will separate from Canada, judgments about equalization payments may have to be conditional, with and without Quebec.

This study has five parts. The first is a brief description of the Canadian program of equalization payments. The second is about equality, about whether the Canadian program of equalization payments succeeds in equalizing the distribution of income among all Canadians. The third part is about efficiency, about whether the national income, broadly defined, is higher with equalization payments than it would otherwise be. The fourth part is about equity, defined for the purposes of this paper as conformity with the community's sense of what is just, right, and fitting in the conduct of public affairs. The fifth part is about reform, how the Canadian equalization formula might usefully be modified and whether the institution is worth preserving at all.[1]

Part I: From Section 36(2) to the Canadian Equalization Formula

IT IS BY NO MEANS OBVIOUS how Section 36(2) is to be translated into a formula specifying which provinces are to receive equalization payments and how large their equalization payments should be. The problem is best approached in stages. Consider first a country with uniform prices of all goods and services nation wide, and with two provinces, A and B, where *all* public revenue, federal and provincial, is raised by proportional income taxation. Suppose the data are as shown in table I.1.

Table I.1: Data for the Calculation of Entitlements to Equalization Payments

Province	Total Provincial Income ($ billion)	Population (million)	Provincial Tax Rate (%)	Revenue from Provincial Taxation ($ billion)
A	100	2	25	25
B	30	1	20	6
A and B	130	3	—	31

Province A is the "have" province with an income per head of $50,000, and province B is the "have not" province with an income per head of $30,000. In this example, the "have" province has the larger population as well as the larger income, but that is not important in the determination of equalization payments. An equalization program in the spirit of Section 36(2) would transfer income, one way or another, from province A to province B. The size of the transfer would presumably depend on the shortfall of revenue in province B, that is, on the extent to which revenue per head would be less in province B than in province A if the tax rates in the two provinces were the same.

The main ingredient of the Canadian equalization formula is the "shortfall in provincial revenue" which is defined for any province i as follows:

$$\begin{pmatrix} average \\ provincial \\ tax\ rate \end{pmatrix} x \left[\begin{pmatrix} average \\ provincial \\ tax\ base \\ per\ head \end{pmatrix} - \begin{pmatrix} tax\ base \\ per\ head \\ province\ i \end{pmatrix} \right] x \begin{pmatrix} population \\ of \\ province\ i \end{pmatrix}$$

where the tax base in the example is income measured as gross domestic product. Converting from words to symbols, the shortfall of revenue in province i, S_i, is defined as

$$S_i = t_c [y_c - y_i] P_i \tag{I.1}$$

where i refers to either province A or province B, C is mnemonic for Canada, and

y_i is income per head in province i (for income is the assumed provincial the tax base),

y_c is income per head in the entire country,

P_i is the population of province i, and

t_c is the average provincial tax rate measured as the ratio of the total provincial tax revenue in both provinces to the total tax base.

The average provincial tax rate is 23.8 percent; it is the total provincial revenue of $31 billion (25 percent of $100 billion plus 20 percent of $30 billion) as a percentage of the total income in both provinces of $130 billion. For province B, the shortfall of revenue as defined in equation I.1 is

$S_B = (0.238)[(130/3) - (30/1)](1)$ billion
   $= \$3.173$ billion

and, for province A, the shortfall is

$S_A = (0.238)[(130/3) - (100/2)](2)$ billion
   $= - \$3.173$ billion

Note that provincial shortfalls cancel out; this remains true for the full Canadian equalization formula.

An additional step is required to convert the shortfall of provincial revenue in each province—positive in province B and negative in province A—into entitlements for equalization payments. There would seem to be two main options, options that extend to the design of the broader formula to be discussed presently. Canada might have adopted a "net" formula according to which the federal government would give or take from each province according to its shortfall of provincial revenue, regardless of whether the shortfall is positive, as in province B, or negative, as in province A. A "have not" province with a positive shortfall would be entitled to an equalization payment. A "have" province with a negative shortfall would be taxed. Taxes and subsidies would be just equal to the shortfalls in the provinces concerned. As for the federal government, its subsidies to the "have not" provinces would just equal its levies from the "have" provinces, and rates of ordinary federal taxation would be unaffected. Specifically, each province's entitlement to an equalization payment, or its levy to finance equalization payments to other provinces, would be E_i where

$$E_i = S_i \qquad\qquad\qquad\qquad\qquad (\text{I}.2)$$

regardless of whether S_i is positive or negative. This method would ensure that provincial revenues per head are equal in all provinces as long as provincial tax rates were the same. Though advocated by some students of equalization payments, this procedure has not been adopted in Canada, perhaps in recognition of the principle that "the crown cannot tax the crown."

Instead, Canada chose to "equalize up," but not down. The federal government covers the shortfall of revenue in the "have not" provinces, but there is no corresponding levy on the "have" provinces, so that the cost of the program must be covered by ordinary federal taxation. Poor provinces are subsidized, but rich provinces are left alone, except in so far as residents of rich provinces, like all citizens, are subject to ordinary taxation by the federal government. Specifically, each province's entitlement to equalization payments would be

$E_i = $ *the larger of* $[0, S_i]$ (I.3)

It is important to recognize that equalization in accordance with equation I.3, and its generalization to more complex situations, is incomplete. Section 36(2) would seem to require the federal government to provide a large enough transfer of income to the poor provinces that their revenue per head, inclusive of equalization payments, would be no less than that of the rich provinces when all provinces impose the same provincial tax rate. The Canadian formula does not quite do that. It subsidizes poor provinces, but does not tax rich provinces directly. A province with a negative shortfall in revenue—that is, with a relatively large tax base per head—receives no equalization payment. A province with a positive shortfall in revenue—that is, with a relatively small tax base per head—receives an equalization payment sufficient to bring its revenue per head (inclusive of equalization payments) up to the average revenue per head (without equalization payments) in all provinces together, but not to full equality with the rich provinces. Of course, residents in rich provinces pay a disproportionate share of the cost of the equalization program because they pay a disproportionate share of the federal tax to finance it.

For our two-province example, the post-equalization finances of the provincial governments are shown in table I.2.

Table I.2: Equalization and Provincial Revenue			
Province	**Revenue from Own Taxation ($ billion)**	**Revenue from Equalization Payment ($ billion)**	**Total Revenue per Head ($ thousand)**
A	25	0.0	12.5
B	6	3.173	9.173

Even with equalization payments, provincial revenues per head are not the same. The magnitude of the difference is, of course, a consequence of numbers that have been chosen arbitrarily, but the presence of some difference is a universal characteristic of the Canadian equalization program. The difference arises from two sources: a) If provincial tax rates were the same, the government of the richer province would acquire a larger revenue per head because, by definition, its tax base per head exceeds the average tax base in the two provinces together; b) If provincial tax bases were the same, the province choosing the higher tax rate would automatically acquire the larger revenue. It is important to recognize that the Canadian program of equalization payments does not mandate equality among provinces of revenue or public services per head.

Construction of the Canadian equalization forumula

Before extending the simple expression for the shortfall of income in equation I.1 to account for the multiplicity of provincial tax bases, it should be recognized that a program of equalization payments could be based on equation I.1 as it stands. Each province's shortfall of revenue could be assessed in accordance with equation I.1 regardless of the multiplicity of actual taxes in each province, the personal income tax, the corporation income tax, property tax, dog licenses and so on. Provinces could be treated *as if* all revenues were raised by income taxation. The average provincial tax rate, t_c, would be measured as the ratio of total provincial revenue in all provinces together to the gross domestic product in Canada as a whole. The "macro formula" in equation I.1 could be coupled with the "net" rule in equation I.2 or the "equalizing up" rule in equation I.3. A number of students of equalization payments, myself included, believe that a macro formula would be preferable, all things considered, to the formula used in Canada today. Canada has chosen instead to take account of the multiplicity of provincial tax bases and to measure provincial shortfalls of tax revenue accordingly. The simple formula in equation I.1 must therefore be generalized. A workable equalization rule must make allowance for the following:

i) There are ten provinces rather than just two. The extension from two to ten provinces is straightforward.

ii) An equalization formula must average over the different sources of tax revenue, for otherwise a strict reading of Section 36(2) gives rise to an inconsistency, and it may be literally impossible for the federal government to do what the Canadian Constitution would seem to require. Suppose that income per head is the same in province A and province B, that tax revenue per head is the same as well, but that the provinces differ in the industrial composition of income and the sources of tax revenue. Let the income in each province be $60,000 per head and the tax revenue be $10,000 per head. Income per head in province A consists of $40,000 from fishing and $20,000 from farming, while income per head in province B is the opposite, $20,000 from fishing and $40,000 from farming. Now suppose that each province imposes a tax on its major industry and leaves the other industry untaxed altogether. Province A levies a 25 percent tax on income from fishing and province B levies a 25 percent tax on income from farming. Financially, the two provinces are exactly alike, but neither can, in the words of Section 36(2), provide reasonably comparable levels of services at reasonably comparable levels of taxation. With the tax structure of province B, revenue in province A would fall from $10,000 to $5,000. With the tax structure of province A, revenue in province B would fall from $10,000 to $5,000. Strictly speaking, both would be deficit provinces entitled to equalization payments. Clearly, in constructing an equalization formula in the spirit of section 36(2), it is necessary to draw a balance for each province between its larger than average endowments of some tax bases and its smaller than average endowments of others.

The Canadian procedure is to recognize 33 distinct tax bases, to aggregate the shortfalls (the sum of the positive shortfalls less the sum of the negative shortfalls) in each province, and then to provide equalization payments according to the aggregate shortfall in each province, as long as the aggregate is positive. The list of tax bases is presented as appendix table I.1.

iii) There is more than one way to calculate the average provincial tax base per head and the average provincial tax rate for each base. The obvious procedure is to measure the average provincial base per head as the total base in all provinces together divided by the total population of Canada, and to measure the average rate as the ratio of the total revenue in all provinces to the aggregate tax base. That was the Canadian procedure until the mid 1970s, but a slightly different procedure is employed now. Now, entitlements to equalization payments are assessed on a "five province average." Though average provincial tax rates are still computed for all 10 provinces, the average provincial tax base is now computed for the five provinces of British Columbia, Saskatchewan, Manitoba, Ontario, and Quebec. Alberta is left out because its revenue from oil was so large at the time when the procedure was changed that every province except Alberta would have been eligible for equalization payments. The Maritime provinces were then left out as well to compensate for the lowering of average entitlements from the exclusion of Alberta.

The Canadian equalization formula becomes

$$E_i = \text{the larger of } [0, \sum_{j=1}^{33} t_{cj} \left(Q_{cj} - Q_{ij} \right) P_i] \tag{I.4}$$

where i refers to one of 10 provinces
j refers to one of 33 provincial taxes
c refers to Canada as a whole

E_i is the entitlement to equalization payments of province i

P_i is the population of province i

t_{cj} is the Canadian average provincial tax rate on base j

Q_{ij} is the base *per head* for tax j in province i and

Q_{cj} is the Canadian average base *per head* for the tax j.

The calculation of entitlements to equalization payments is based on 670 supposedly primary statistics, populations of the 10 provinces, dollar values of revenues for each of the 33 provincial taxes and each of the 10 provinces, and dollar values or quantities, as the case may be, of tax bases for each of the 33 taxes and each of the 10 provinces. Specifically, the primary data are

population (i) for i = 1 to 10,

tax base (i,j) for i = 1 to 10 and j = 1 to 33,

and revenue (i,j) for i = 1 to 10 and j = 1 to 33.

Then, for each tax, the base per head in each province, the base per head in Canada as a whole, and the average provincial rate in Canada as a whole are

$$Q_{ij} = tax\ base\ (i,\ j)/population\ (i)$$

$$Q_{cj} = \sum_{i=1}^{5} tax\ base\ (i,\ j)\ /\ \sum_{i=1}^{5} population\ (i)$$

where the summations are over the provinces of Quebec, Ontario, Manitoba, Saskatchewan and British Columbia, and

$$t_{cj} = \sum_{i=1}^{10} revenue\ (i,\ j)\ /\ \sum_{i=1}^{10} base\ (i,\ j)$$

where the summations are over all 10 provinces. The dimension of t_{cj} is a reflection of the choice of the tax base. If the base is measured in dollars in the first instance, then the rate is automatically pure number like a percent. If the base is measured as a quantity in the first instance, then the rate is automatically expressed in dollars per unit. Income taxes and sales taxes (items 1 and 4 in appendix table 1) exemplify the first procedure. Tobacco taxes and gasoline taxes (items 5 and 6) exemplify the second.

Problems of measurement

There is an unavoidable element of discretion in the selection and interpretation of the primary data. First, the Canadian formula is automatically biased against provinces with high price levels. This is true for all of the equalization formulas we have been considering, but the problem is most easily illustrated for the macro formula in equation I.1 coupled with the equalizing-up rule in equation I.3. In the application of the formula, a province with a large dollar value of income per head is deemed to be a "have" province, regardless of whether money income is large because prices are high or because residents in the province are prosperous. Suppose there are only two provinces which are identical except that the price level in province A is *twice* the price level in province B. Each province has a population of one million, the common provincial tax rate is 20 percent, the income per head in province A is $40,000 and the income per head in province B is $20,000. Clearly, since people in both provinces are equally well off, it is contrary to the spirit of Section 36(2) to provide equalization payments to either province. Nevertheless, mistaking high prices for high incomes, the Canadian equalization programme would supply a transfer of $2 billion, (.2)[30,000 - 20,000] (1,000,000), to province B, financed by federal taxation in the country as a whole.

The example is not altogether fanciful. Transportation costs do cause price levels to differ from place to place. Though price level differences among the Canadian provinces are much less pronounced than in the example, there is a large price gap between the Canadian north and the rest of the country. That is perhaps a reason why federal transfers to the Yukon and the Northwest Territories are not in accordance with the Canadian equalization formula.

Second, entitlement to equalization is not independent of the choice of the tax base. To focus clearly on the pitfalls in the choice of the tax base, imagine a country with only two provinces, Ontario and Manitoba, where all provincial revenue is acquired by a tax on dog licenses and where the base of the tax in both provinces is the number of dogs. In accordance with equation (I.4), the shortfall of revenue in province i is $t_{cj}(Q_{cj} - Q_{ij})P_i$ where j refers to the tax on dog licenses, Q_{ij} is the number of dogs per person in province i, t_{cj} is the average tax rate in the two provinces together and Q_{cj} is the average number of dogs per head. With only two provinces, there can be at most one recipient of equalization payments, the province for which $(Q_{cj} - Q_{ij})$ is positive. Since the dog tax is the only source of provincial revenue, a province's entitlement to equalization payment is the value of this expression if and only if it is positive. Thus an equalization payment is paid to whichever province has the smaller number of dogs per head. This outcome is reasonable as long as the quality of dogs in the two provinces is more or less the same. If there are more dogs per person in Manitoba than in Ontario, then Ontario becomes the "have not" province and is the recipient of an equalization payment.

The procedure becomes problematic when the provincial tax base is a poor representation of the economic activity in the province. Suppose people in Ontario and Manitoba keep different breeds of dogs. Suppose Ontario contains a small number of expensive poodles, Manitoba contains a large number of inexpensive mutts, and the *value* of dogs is larger in Ontario than in Manitoba. With the number of dogs as the tax base (with Q_{ij} measured as the number of dogs per head in province i), Ontario remains as the recipient of equalization payments despite the fact that it has the larger dollar value of the tax base in the two provinces. Worse still, Ontario appears increasingly disadvantaged the higher its dog tax happens to be, for t_{cj} in the formula is the average dog tax in both provinces together. The classier its dogs, and the higher its dog tax, the larger Ontario's entitlement to equalization payments would become. Such anomalies tend to cancel out when there are many provinces and many tax bases, but the problem does not disappear altogether.

If breeds really differed among provinces as in this deliberately far-fetched example, the natural tax base for the equalization formula would be value rather than quantity; Q_{ij} would be measured in the first instance as the value of dogs j in province i rather than as the number, the term $(Q_{cj} - Q_{ij})$ would be positive for Manitoba rather than for Ontario, and Manitoba would become the "have not" province entitled to equalization payments. Alternatively, poodles and mutts might be recognized as distinct tax bases, in which case Manitoba might, once again, be the recipient province. On the other hand, if the provinces assessed dogs taxes as *dollars per dog*, if records were kept of the number of dogs and the revenue from the dog tax but not of the price or value of dogs, and if evidence about differences in breeds among provinces were just anecdotal, then the Department of Finance would have little choice but to assess the base of the dog tax as a number of dogs. The problem is compounded if prices of all breeds of dogs are higher in one province than in another, a consideration which, taken by itself, points to quantity rather than value as the appropriate base. Provinces may differ in the manner of taxation. Ontario may impose different taxes on poodles and mutts, while Manitoba may impose the same tax on all breeds. Poodle prices may depend on the pedigrees of the dogs. Tastes for the different breeds may vary between provinces.

The point of this example is not that the Canadian equalization formula is unworkable, but that it is not altogether free of statistical judgment. Like virtually all statistically-grounded rules, it leaves room for dispute at the margin as to how it should be applied, and interested parties have incentives to favour this or that interpretation. Presumably, in this case, shrewd statisticians would be content to say that a dog is a dog is a dog.

Nor is this measurement problem as far-fetched as the dog example might suggest, for it appears with a vengeance in the identification of the revenue base of the property tax. One might, of course, suppose that an acre is an acre is an acre, but that would be altogether unsatisfactory because an acre of land in the Prairies is worth very much less than an acre of land in Toronto. Such a rule would make residents of Toronto appear land-poor (and would signify a shortfall of potential property tax revenue) when the residents of Toronto may, in fact, be land rich, especially if the value of structures is taken into account.

The difficulty is compounded by a marked variation among provinces in the ascription values of land and structures for the assessment of property tax. Some jurisdictions use market-based assessments, others use historical values that may be entirely artificial and unrepresentative of current prices. Apparently there is no universally-accepted information on land-and-structures values by the provinces to serve as primary data in the assessment of entitlements to equalization payments. Instead, there has evolved an elaborate procedure in which land values are represented by other provincial characteristics. In applying the equalization formula, the base of the property tax is estimated in three parts: farm land, commercial property, and residential property. The value of farm land is measured directly. The value of commercial property is estimated as a multiple of "adjusted" gross domestic product in the province. The value of residential property is estimated as a multiple of "adjusted" personal income in the province. Details of the estimation occupy half a dozen impenetrable pages in *The Canada Gazette*.[2] It should be stressed that, though much of the primary data in the equalization formula is uncomfortably judgmental, the entitlements are not necessarily biased or wrong on that account.

Even more disturbing is the possible dependence of tax base on tax rate. The Canadian equalization formula rests on an implicit assumption that the revenue base is what it is, regardless of the chosen tax rate. That assumption is invariably false, to a greater or lesser degree. Any tax imposes a spread between the post-tax price and the pre-tax price of the taxed good. Either the post-tax price rises, or the pre-tax price falls, or both. The effects of taxes on prices presents no difficulty for the equalization formula if the pre-tax value of a tax base is invariant, and if the pre-tax value is employed as the measure of the tax base, or, alternatively, if the post-tax value is invariant and the post-tax value is employed as the measure of the tax base. Problems arise when the chosen base is not invariant, as, for instance, when the market value of land serves as the base of the property tax. An increase in a province's property tax lowers the value of land in the province, making the province appear land-poor and increasing its entitlement to equalization payments. Property taxation is the most egregious example of this phenomenon.

Of less importance is a comparable impact on quantities. Taxpayers always seek to minimize liability for tax by redirecting effort from highly taxed to less taxed activities. The income tax diverts time from paid work to leisure or do-it-yourself activities. The excise tax on cigarettes reduces smoking or encourages smuggling. Such manoeuvres cause the base of any tax to shrink as the rate increases, affecting entitlements to equalization payments. It is uncertain to what extent each province's entitlement is affected. The Canadian equalization program departs from equations I.3 and I.4 by a number of ad hoc constraints and adjustments. There are "ceiling and floor" constraints on the extent to which a province's entitlement can be increased or decreased in any year. There is also a "tax-back" rule, to be discussed in some detail in the chapter on equity. The equalization formula is adjusted in special circumstances where a recipient province has so large a share of some particular tax base that revenue raised by taxation on that base conveys almost no advantage to the province because there would be an almost dollar-for-dollar reduction in the province's entitlement to equalization payments.

Finally, the reader should note a subtle difference in the definitions of shortfall in provincial revenue in equations I.1 and I.4. The average provincial tax rate in equation I.1 is computed from information about the finances of provinces A and B as they would be without the equalization program. That is not quite the procedure in the Canadian program. The Canadian procedure, as described in equation I.4, is to set the average provincial tax rates, t_{cj}, as they are observed to be with the equalization program in place. The value of t_c in the in the example in tables I.1 and I.2 was 23.8 percent. Following the Canadian procedure, t_c would be somewhat lower and the equalization payment would be correspondingly lower as well, but the story would be essentially the same. The procedure in equation I.4 was chosen for its simplicity; otherwise, the average provincial tax rate would have to be estimated by iteration.

The size of the Canadian equalization program

For the year 1994, the equalization program is summarized in tables I.3, I.4 and I.5. Table I.3 sets the scene with data by province of the dollar values of the equalization payments to the recipient provinces, together with total federal transfers to all provinces, provincial gross domestic product per head, population and provincial shares of the revenue from the federal income tax. Then table I.4 shows equalization per head by province, together with total federal transfers per head and net payments per head over and above the cost to the residents of each province of the extra federal taxation that would be required to finance the entire program if federal revenue were acquired by income taxation. The total

Table I.3: Equalization Payments and Total Transfers to the Provinces, 1994

Province	(1) Population (Thousands)	(2) Gross Domestic Product per Head (Dollars)	(3) Equalization Payments (Millions of Dollars)	(4) Total Transfers from the Federal Gov't (Millions of Dollars)	(5) Shares of Federal Income Tax
Canada	29,219.2	25,620	7,980	26,619	1.000000
Nfld	582.2	16,710	904	1,423	0.012192
P.E.I.	134.4	18,061	170	291	0.002947
N.S.	936.2	19,678	869	1,612	0.025651
N.B.	758.9	19,773	879	1,574	0.018405
Que.	7,275.8	22,965	3,768	7,791	0.216889
Ont.	10,919.4	27,663		7,057	0.434501
Man.	1,129.7	22,213	867	1,863	0.030508
Sask.	1,015.2	22,839	523	1,526	0.026217
Alta.	2,712.6	30,310		2,868	0.097713
B.C.	3,660.8	27,289		2,268	0.128724
Yukon	30.0	30,433		356	0.001067
N.W.T.	64.2	30,502		991	0.002393

Sources: (1) and (2) *CANSIM*, Statistics Canada; (3) *The Equalization Program 1994-95*. Federal-Provincial Relations Division. Department of Finance, April 1994; (4) *Public Sector Finance 1994-95*, Statistics Canada, #68-212, table 1.28. Data for 1993/94 fiscal year; (5) *Taxation Statistics*, Revenue Canada 1993, Basic Table 1. Data for 1992, the most recent year available.

Table I.4: Equalization Payments and Transfers per Person, 1994

Province	(1) Equalization Payments (Dollars per Person)	(2) Net Gain (or Loss) from Equalization Payments (Dollars per Person)	(3) Transfers from the Federal Government (Dollars per Person)	(4) Net Gain (or Loss) from Federal Transfers (Dollars per Person)
Canada	273.12	0.00	1013.69	0.00
Nfld.	1553.01	1,385.90	2,444.24	1,823.92
P.E.I.	1,264.37	1,089.35	2,162.60	1,515.70
N.S.	928.30	709.65	1,722.13	910.32
N.B.	1,157.73	964.19	2,074.32	1,355.72
Quebec	517.92	280.03	1,070.76	187.88
Ontario	0.00	(317.55)	646.33	(532.31)
Manitoba	767.41	551.89	1,648.92	849.23
Sask.	515.48	309.39	1,503.39	738.25
Alberta	0.00	(287.47)	1,057.20	(9.64)
B.C.	0.00	(280.61)	619.41	(422.20)
Yukon	0.00	(283.83)	11,876.67	10,813.22
N.W.T.	0.00	(297.34)	15,423.90	14,287.61

Note: the numbers in brackets are losses.

Sources: (1) The ratio of columns 1 and 3 in table I.3.
(2) Numbers in each row are the values of $E_i - t_i E_C$, where E_i is the equalization to province i (column 1 of table I.3), E_C is the total equalization to all provinces and t_i is the tax share of province i (column 5 of table I.3).
(3) Ratio of columns 4 and 1 of table I.3.
(4) Same as column 2 except that equalization payments are replaced by total transfers (column 4 of table I.3).

cost of the equalization program was 8 billion dollars of which just under half, 3.8 billion dollars, was for Quebec, another 2.8 billion dollars was for the Maritime provinces and 1.4 billion dollars was for Manitoba and Saskatchewan. But the largest payments per head were in the Maritimes where the income per head is low. Payment per head was $1,553 in Newfoundland and $518 in Quebec. Net payments are, of course lower in the recipient provinces and negative in the donor provinces of Ontario, Alberta, and British Columbia, which receive no equalization payments but pay substantial shares of the federal tax to finance them. The cost of the program to the residents of Ontario was $318 per head. In the federal budget of 1995, total equalization payments are predicted to rise to 9.3 billion dollars.

Finally, table I.5 summarizes the entire cost of the equalization program since its inception in 1957. The table is constructed from the time-series in appendix table 2 of equalization payments by province from the beginning of the program until the most recent year for which data is available. Each of the five columns of the table is for a different measure of the size of the program. The first column is the sum of all payments from 1957 to 1994, converted into 1994 dollars by the consumer price index. The numbers are deflated because a dollar of transfer in 1957 represented very different amounts of goods and services in 1957 than in 1994. The remaining columns show alternative measures of "debt-equivalents." The idea of a debt equivalent is to assess the size of a program that has been in operation for some time as the amount by which the Canadian national debt would be smaller today if the program had not existed at all. Each of these measures is constructed on the supposition that there were no equalization payments but that all federal taxes, tax revenues, and other expenditures remained as they were. On that supposition, the deficit each year would have been reduced by the amount of the equalization payments. Then, since the federal government must pay interest on its debt, the debt-equivalent of the equalization payments in any given year would grow year by year according to the rate of interest that the federal government must pay. The numbers in the last four columns of table I.5 are the sum for each province of the debt-equivalents for every year that the program was in force. It is by no means obvious what rate of interest is appropriate for this calculation because different components of government debt bear different rates of interest in any given year, and because actual rates would have been different, and probably slightly lower, had the debt been smaller than it actually was. Thus, debt-equivalents are calculated for four alternative assumptions about the rate of interest by which debts are assumed to accumulate. In the second column, the assumed rate is for 90-day Treasury bills, which is probably a bit too low. The next column adds 1 percent, the next an additional percent, and the final

Table I.5: Alternative Measures of the Cost since its Inception of the Canadian Equalization Program ($ billion)

Recipient Provinces	The Sum of All Expenditures in $ 1994	Debt Equivalents			
		At the Rate on 90-day Treasury Bills	Treasury Bill Rate +1%	Treasury Bill Rate +2%	Treasury Bill Rate +3%
Nfld.	21.3	35.7	40.7	46.7	53.9
P.E.I.	4.7	8.1	9.2	10.7	12.4
N.S.	23.4	40.0	46.0	53.0	61.6
N.B.	20.8	35.0	40.0	46.0	53.2
Quebec	96.6	164.7	187.8	215.1	247.6
Manitoba	18.1	29.8	33.7	38.3	43.7
Sask.	8.8	13.9	16.3	19.2	22.8
Alta.	0.5	1.1	1.5	2.1	2.9
B.C.	0.2	0.4	0.5	0.7	1.0
Total	194.5	328.8	375.9	432.0	499.1

Source: Appendix table 2. British Columbia and Alberta received small equalization payments in the 1950s.

column accumulates debt at the 90-day Treasury bill rate plus 3 percent which is, I suspect, too high.[3]

Part II: Equality

T HE NAME "EQUALIZATION PAYMENTS" is, to say the least, suggestive. From the name alone, one would automatically suppose the Canadian program to narrow the distribution of income in Canada, making the poor become richer and the rich become poorer than they would otherwise be. Or, confusing provinces with people, one might suppose that equalization among provinces is desirable in itself, regardless of the identities of the ultimate gainers and losers from the program. Equalization payments must equalize incomes, for how else could the program serve as the embodiment of the great ideals and great values of Canadians, the underpinning of the unique sense of Canadian sharing and the assurance that no citizen of Canada is second class?

But the consequences of programs are not bound by the connotations of words. The name of a program cannot predetermine its impact on the distribution of income in Canada or guarantee that the program is equalizing among people at all. The Canadian program of equalization payments is a transfer from the federal government to the governments of certain provinces, chosen because their tax bases are less than the national average. The transfer may narrow the distribution of income in Canada to some extent, but it will, almost certainly, lead to a decrease in the incomes some poor people and to an increase in the incomes of some rich people. Any transfer of income from the federal government to selected provinces would

   i)   enable the governments of the recipient provinces to increase expenditure, reduce tax rates or both,

ii) require the federal government to increase tax rates, reduce other expenditure or both,

iii) induce governments of the donor provinces—provinces not favoured with transfers from the federal governments but whose residents must bear a share of the cost of transfers in their tax bill from the federal government—to alter patterns of taxation and expenditure

iv) provide incentives for citizens in all provinces to modify their behaviour—where to locate, where to invest, how much labour to supply and what to buy—in response to all of the changes in taxation and public expenditure.

Initially, attention is focused on the behaviour of governments; only afterwards are the citizen's responses taken into account.

But not even within the narrow frame of reference can the full impact of a program of equalization payments upon the incomes of citizens be definitively predicted. For example, the distribution of income in Canada would be narrowed by a program of equalization payments if the recipient provinces were induced to increase expenditure for the homeless, and if the federal government acquired the extra revenue to finance the program by an increase in taxation on the wealthy. On the other hand, the distribution of income would be widened if the recipient provinces chose to reduce property taxes, and if the federal government covered the cost of equalization payments by a reduction in assistance to the unemployed. As one cannot say for certain which of these combinations, or of a thousand other possible combinations, will be realized, one must recognize that it is virtually impossible to provide a definitive identification of the beneficiaries of the program. The chain of causation from equalization payments to the welfare of the poor is hard, bordering on impossible, to follow. The best I can do is to sort out some of the possibilities in a series of examples, beginning with one where equalization payments really are equalizing among people and then proceeding to others where the main beneficiaries of the program are not poor, or where the ultimate effect of the program may be to transfer income from the poor to the rich.

A transfer from rich people to poor people

This example may be in the back of the minds of those who see the Canadian program as the great manifestation of our democracy and of our compassion as a nation. The example is a slight variant of the illustration of the equalization formula in tables I.1 and I.2. There are two provinces, A and B, each with a population of one million. People's incomes are equal within each province but unequal across provinces. Everybody in province A has an income of $20,000; everybody in province B has an income of $5,000. The main difference between this example and the example in table I.1 is that there is now assumed to be a fixed requirement for public expenditure. Both provinces are confronted with an overhead cost of $1,000 per head and must set provincial tax rates to supply the required tax revenue. The effects of equalization payments are shown in table II.1, which is largely self-explanatory.

Table II.1: The Financial Consequence of Equalization Payments with Proportional Income Taxation by the Provinces and by the Federal Government (Each province spends $1,000 per head)

Prov.	Gross Income per Head ($)	Without Equalization Payments		With Equalization Payments			Net Gain from Equalization Payments ($ per head)
		Provincial Tax Rate	Net Income per Head ($)	Provincial Tax Rate	Federal Tax Rate	Net Income per Head ($)	
A	20,000	5%	19,000	5%	2.4%	18,520	-480
B	5,000	20%	4,000	8%	2.4%	4,480	+480
Avg.	12,500	8%	11,500	5.6%	2.4%	11,500	—

The average income per head is $12,500 [(20,000 + 5,000)/2], and the average provincial tax rate in the absence of equalization payments is 8 percent. A routine application of the equalization formula in equations I.1 and I.3 provides an equalization payment of $600 million to province B, which is poor, and nothing to province A, which is rich. Denote income per head in province B by y_B, average income per head by Y_C, the population of province B by P_B, the average provincial tax rate denoted by t_C and the equalization payment to province B by E_B. The equalization payment becomes

$$E_B = (t_C)(y_C - y_B)P_B$$
$$= (.08)(\$12,500 - \$5,000)(1,000,000)$$
$$= \$\ 600\ million\ or\ \$600\ per\ head$$

With a national tax base of $25 billion, the federal government can finance an equalization payment of $600 million by a nation-wide income tax at a rate of 2.4 percent. With an equalization payment of $600 per head, province B can finance its required expenditure of $1,000 per head by a provincial tax rate of only 8 percent which is, by construction, the average provincial tax rate in the absence of equalization payments. Thus the net effect of a program of equalization payments is to equalize provincial tax rates, but not completely. The total, federal and provincial, tax rate rises from 5 percent to 7.4 percent [5 + 2.4] on residents in province A, and falls from 20 percent to 10.4 percent [8 + 2.4] on residents in province B. The total after-tax income per head falls from $19,000 to $18,520 in province A and rises from $4,000 to $4,482 in province B. There is, on balance, a net transfer of income of $480 per head from province A to province B, constituting an unambiguous narrowing of the income distribution in the nation as a whole. The poorer province is still unable to supply the same public services as the richer province at the same rate of taxation, but there is a significant step in that direction.

Bear in mind, however, that the example is based on the very strong assumption that public services are a fixed overhead cost which must be borne if the province is to function at all. This assumption is never completely valid but it is more nearly so for some public services than for others, more nearly so for the roads than for parks or museums.

When public services are a fixed overhead cost, the ultimate effect of equalization payments is entirely upon purchases of private goods and services in the provinces. But when public services are not a fixed overhead cost, poor provinces would be inclined to spend less than rich provinces, leaving their taxpayers with more money for private goods and services. In practice, equalization payments might be expected to influence the provision of public services in the different provinces to a greater or lesser extent.

A transfer from rich people in the rich province to rich people in the poor province

The story changes significantly when we drop the assumption that everybody within a province is alike. It was assumed in table II.1 that absolutely everybody in province A has an income of $20,000 per year and that absolutely everybody in province B has an income of $5,000 per year. The assumption is unrealistic in two respects: The fourfold gap between the incomes per head in the two provinces is far too large. Gross domestic product per head does not differ among Canadian provinces to anything like that extent. In fact, the largest gap between provinces— the gap between Alberta and Newfoundland—is only 77 percent of the income of the poorer province. Second, and more important, the difference between a rich province and a poor province is not that everybody in one province is rich and everybody in the other is poor. The difference is that the proportion of rich people is larger in one province than in the other. With intra-provincial—as distinct from inter-provincial—variation in income, a program of equalization payments may transfer incomes among rich people rather than between rich people and poor people.

For Canada and for each province, the distribution of income in 1993 is shown in Table II.2. The table shows that every province contains people in every income range, though of course, the proportion of rich people is high in rich provinces and low in poor provinces. The significance of the table for the assessment of the Canadian program of equalization payments is that there would seem to be enough rich people in poor provinces and enough poor people in rich provinces that

Table II.2: Percentage Distribution of Families and Unattached Individuals by Income Groups and Provinces, 1993

Income Group	Cda.	Nfld.	P.E.I.	N.S.	N.B.	Que.	Ont.	Man.	Sask.	Alta.	B.C.
Under $10,000	7.3	8.0	7.5	7.5	6.7	8.9	5.4	7.2	7.2	8.0	8.8
$10,000-14,999	10.5	11.7	11.8	12.3	12.6	12.3	8.7	11.1	3.0	9.8	10.6
15,000-19,999	8.4	9.4	9.0	9.9	8.1	9.0	8.0	9.5	8.0	7.8	7.7
20,000-24,999	8.2	7.7	9.7	9.2	9.1	7.7	8.1	9.8	9.5	8.2	8.3
25,000-29,999	7.2	8.6	12.0	7.8	7.3	8.1	6.8	8.0	9.0	6.3	6.1
30,000-34,999	6.9	8.7	7.4	6.8	6.0	7.2	6.7	6.9	6.8	7.0	6.8
35,000-39,999	6.5	7.0	7.0	7.0	7.8	7.5	6.0	6.1	6.5	6.3	6.1
40,000-44,999	5.6	7.5	6.6	6.9	6.2	5.4	5.3	5.9	6.0	5.6	5.9
45,000-49,999	5.4	5.4	6.2	5.4	6.3	5.7	5.2	5.1	5.6	5.0	5.9
50,000-54,999	4.7	4.1	4.1	4.9	5.2	4.4	4.6	5.7	4.0	4.1	5.3
55,000-59,999	4.8	4.6	3.0	4.6	4.4	4.6	5.0	3.9	4.5	5.2	4.4
60,000-64,999	3.7	3.5	3.9	3.0	3.6	3.2	3.9	3.9	3.4	4.5	4.1

Table II.2 (continued)

Income Group	Cda.	Nfld.	P.E.I.	N.S.	N.B.	Que.	Ont.	Man.	Sask.	Alta.	B.C.
70,000-74,999	3.0	2.7	1.8	2.3	2.8	2.6	3.3	2.8	2.6	3.4	3.0
75,000-79,999	2.4	1.4	1.5	1.7	2.6	1.9	3.0	1.7	2.0	3.0	2.2
80,000-89,999	3.8	2.9	2.2	1.9	3.5	3.4	4.8	3.3	3.2	3.6	3.2
90,000-99,999	2.7	1.6	2.0	1.5	2.3	2.0	3.6	1.7	2.3	2.8	2.6
100,000 & over	5.6	2.6	2.0	4.7	2.8	3.4	7.8	4.0	3.5	5.8	6.0
Total	100.0	100.0	100.0	100.0	100.0	100.0	100.0	100.0	100.0	100.0	100.0
Average Income	$43,880	$37,940	$36,309	$39,256	$39,906	$38,816	$48,747	$40,420	$39,248	$45,590	$44,221
Median Income	$36,109	$32,635	$29,977	$32,449	$35,166	$32,787	$40,145	$33,130	$32,351	$37,204	$36,214

Source: *Income Distribution by Size in Canada*, 1993, Annual, Statistics Canada #13-207, table 34.

the effects of the program could conceivably be perverse. Much of the potential benefit to the poor might be siphoned off by the rich in the recipient provinces, much of the cost may be borne by the poor in the rich province, and the program may in the end fail to be equalizing at all.

How this might come about is illustrated in Table II.3 which is a variant of a famous example by James Buchanan.[4] A country contains two provinces A and B, and six people, three rich and three poor. Each rich person has a gross, pre-tax income of $10,000 per year, and each poor person has a gross, pre-tax income of $1,000 per year. Of the rich, two live in province A and one lives in province B. Of the poor, one lives in province A and two live in province B. Specifically, the three people in province A are A1, A2, and A3 with incomes of $10,000, $10,000 and $1,000 respectively, and the three people in province B are B1, B2, and B3 with incomes of $10,000, $1,000 and $1,000 respectively. The circumstances of each person are shown in a separate row. The tax base in province A is $21,000 ($10,000 for each of the two rich people and $1,000 for the one poor person) or $7,000 per head. The tax base in province B is $12,000 ($10,000 for the one rich person and $1,000 for each of the two poor people) or $4,000 per head. The total provincial tax base is $33,000 or $5,500 per head (33,000/6). All revenue, federal and provincial, is obtained by proportional income taxation at whatever rates are necessary to finance the required public expenditure. In the absence of equalization payments, provincial expenditure in both provinces together is assumed to be $6,000, so that the average provincial tax rate, t_C, must be 18.2 percent (6/33).

Province B is the "have not" province and is entitled, in accordance with the equalization formula in equations I.1 and I.3, to an equalization payment of $818. Specifically, its entitlement is

$$E_B = t_C (y_C - y_B)P_B$$
$$= (.182)($5,500 - $4,000)(3) = $818$$

which is the product of the average provincial tax rate, the shortfall in tax base per head of province B and the population of province B. The federal tax rate to finance the program of equalization payments is 2.48 percent (818/33,000). So far, the example is the same in both parts of Table II.3.

The equalization payment is to the government of the poor province. Whether the benefits of the program accrue to poor people depends critically on how the government of the recipient province responds. The two cases in Table II.3 are designed to demonstrate extreme possibilities. In case (i), provincial tax rates remain unchanged, expenditure in province B is increased and equalization payments are primarily a transfer from rich people in rich provinces to poor people in poor provinces. In case (ii), provincial expenditure is unchanged, the provincial tax rate must fall in province B and equalization payments are primarily a transfer from rich people in rich provinces to rich people in poor provinces.

In case (i), where provincial tax rates are unchanged, the common provincial tax rate is assumed to be 18.2 percent which is just sufficient to provide $6,000 of revenue in both provinces together. At this rate, the "have" province, A, provides each of its residents with $1,273 worth of services, and the "have not" province, B, provides each of its residents with $727 worth of services. The equalization payment enables province B to increase services from $727 to $1,000 per head, which is the average in both provinces together as it would be in the absence of equalization payments. Finally, the income tax levied by the federal government to finance the program of equalization payments places a burden of $248 on each rich person and $25 on each poor person, regardless of one's place of residence. Net gains and losses are shown in the final column of the table. It is immediately evident that the big winners are the poor in province B and the big losers are the rich in province A. The one poor person in province A becomes somewhat worse off, and the one rich person in province B becomes somewhat better off. The tendency in this case is for equalization payments to be equalizing, but not universally so.

In case (ii), where provincial expenditures per head are unchanged. the common provincial expenditure is assumed to be $1,000 per head, or $3,000 altogether, with or without equalization payments. To finance this expenditure in the absence of equalization payments, the "have" province, A, imposes a provincial income tax at a rate of 14.3 percent (3/21), and the "have not" province, B, imposes a tax of 25 percent (3/12). The effect of the equalization payment is now to enable province

Table II.3: The Influence of Equalization Payments on the Distribution of Income

Case (i): Transfer from *Rich* People in the *Rich* Province to *Poor* People in the *Poor* Province. Provincial Tax Rates Invariant at 18.2 Percent (The equalization payment of $818 leads to an increase in public expenditure in the recipient province.)

People	Gross Income	Provincial Tax Rate	Without Equalization Payments — Provincial Public Expenditure	With Equalization Payments — Provincial Public Expenditure	Federal Tax (at 2.48%)	Net Gain
A1	10,000	18.2%	1,273	1,273	248	-248
A2	10,000	18.2%	1,273	1,273	248	-248
A3	1,000	18.2%	1,237	1,273	25	-25
B1	10,000	18.2%	727	1,000	248	25
B2	1,000	18.2%	727	1,000	25	248
B3	1,000	18.2%	727	1,000	25	248
Total	33,000		6,000		818	0

Table II.3 (continued)

Case (ii): Transfer from *Rich* People in the *Rich* Province to *Rich* People in the *Poor* Province
Provincial Expenditure Invariant at $1000 per head
(The equalization payment of $818 leads to a reduction of the provincial tax rate in the recipient province)

People	Gross Income	Without Equalization Payments		With Equalization Payments			
		Provincial Tax Rate	Net Income	Provincial Tax Rate	Federal Tax Rate	Net Income	Net Gain
A1	10,000	14.3%	8,571	14.3%	2.48%	8,323	-248
A2	10,000	14.3%	8,571	14.3%	2.48%	8,323	-248
A3	1,000	14.3%	857	14.3%	2.48%	832	-25
B1	10,000	25%	7,500	18.2%	2.48%	7,934	+434
B2	1,000	25%	750	18.2%	2.48%	793	+43
B3	1,000	25%	750	18.2%	2.48%	793	+43
Total	33,000		27,000			27,000	0

B to lower its tax rate from 25 percent to 18.2 percent, which is the average provincial tax rate as it would be without equalization payments. With a federal income tax rate of 2.48 percent to finance the equalization payment, there is a rise in the combined federal and provincial rate on residents of province A from 14.3 percent to 16.5 percent, and there is a fall in the combined rate on residents of province B from 25 percent to 20.7 percent. The final column in the table shows the net gains and losses to each of the six people in this society. Once again, equalization payments convey a benefit to everybody in province B and a cost to everybody in province A, but the distribution of benefits is very different than in case (i).

The big losers are the same as before, the rich in province A, but now the big winner is the one rich person in province B whose income increases by $434. The net incomes of the two poorest people, B2 and B3, increase by $43 (from $750 to $793), but the net income of the remaining poor person, A3, whose pre-tax income is the same as those of B2 and B3 and whose post-tax income is only slightly larger, falls by $25 (from $857 to $832). The equalization payment of $818 to the poor province generates a total transfer of only $61 from all rich people to all poor people—$43 to each poor person in province B and $25 from the poor person in province A. Meagre transfers to and among the poor are procured by substantial transfers among the rich. This is hardly surprising. As transfers among taxpayers, equalization payments are likely to provide costs and benefits in proportion to the amount of tax one pays.

Do equalization payments promote equality in this example? They may do so, but at best imperfectly. If the aim of a program of equalization payments were to favour poor people, one would have to conclude on the basis of this example that the program is ill-designed, for the revenue of $818 acquired by a federal income taxation at a rate of 2.48 percent would be of greater benefit to the poor if it were transferred directly. The $818 of federal revenue would be sufficient to finance a transfer of $273 to every poor person, for a net gain of $248 after allowance for the $25 tax burden of federal income taxation. In the favourable case, case (i), only two out of three poor people do that well and the third is made somewhat worse off. In the unfavourable case, case (ii), no poor person does nearly that well and, once again, the poor person in the rich province is harmed. In the latter case, there would be some trickling down from the gains to the rich in poor provinces under a program of equalization payments, but that is likely to be small by comparison with the potential gains from direct grants to the poor.

One cannot even be sure that the poorest of the poor will gain at all. As the example is constructed, there is an increase in the minimal post-tax income of any person in the country, but even this paltry equalization among people could be reversed by minor changes in the numbers. Had the pre-tax income of A3 been $500 rather than $1,000, the equalization payment would still have been to province B, but the worst off person, A3, would have become even poorer than before. The example is not entirely fictitious. A donor province may contain some people who are very poor and others who are very rich, rich enough that their province's tax base per head exceeds the national average. An equalization program would then constitute a nation-wide transfer to the middle class from both the rich and the poor. The program would have failed if and in so far as it is intended to improve the lot of the very poor.

The example in table II.3 draws upon the redistributive potential of ordinary income taxation. When a rich person and a poor person buy train tickets, they pay the same price per ticket. When a rich person and a poor person "buy" equal amounts of publicly-provided services at equal rates of taxation, they pay the same share of their incomes, so that, by definition, the rich pay more money and the poor pay less. If private goods were provided like public services, the rich people in the example, A1, A2 and B1, would have to pay ten times the price that is charged to the poor people, A3, B2 and B3.

A program of equalization payments may be looked upon as an incomplete replication within a federal system of government of the financial consequences of a unitary state. In the absence of provinces—if all six people belonged to one and the same jurisdiction, with a total public expenditure of $6,000 and a uniform tax rate on all incomes to cover the cost of public expenditure—the common tax rate would have to be 18.2 percent. The program of equalization payments is a partial reproduction of this state of affairs. The provincial tax rate in the recipient province is reduced to what would be required to finance public services in both provinces by a federal income tax, but the combined federal and provincial tax rate remains higher in the recipient province because federal income taxation to finance equalization payments is imposed on people in both provinces. With any given pre-tax income, one remains better off in the rich province, though less so than without the equalization program. To replicate the complete financial implications of a unitary state, a program of equalization payments would have to supply a larger transfer to the poor province than would be warranted under the Canadian procedure or would have to tax the rich province for the benefit of the poor. Conversion of the equalization program from the equalizing-up rule in equation I.3 to the net rule in equation I.2 would be a substantial step in that direction.

Another critical assumption in the example in table II.3 is that price levels in the two provinces are the same. Were that not so, the Canadian formula in equations I.1 and I.3, which equalizes money incomes rather than real incomes, could easily transfer income from poor provinces to the rich provinces, unintentionally widening the gap between those who are really rich and those who are really poor. Even within the example and despite its huge postulated gap between the incomes of the rich and the poor, the loss of income to person A3 would constitute a lowering of the income of the worst off person in the country if, for instance, the price index were 20 percent higher in province A than in province B. A similar problem arises if, by virtue of its location or the nature of its economy, province A requires a larger public expenditure than province B for a given level of services, as when a sparsely-settled province requires substantial expenditure on transportation. In these cases, it becomes less likely that a program of equalization payments serves to narrow the distribution of real income in the country as a whole.

To summarize the lessons of the example in table II.3, by transferring incomes from rich provinces to poor provinces, a program of equalization payments may, but need not, transfer incomes from rich to poor people. It may be no more than a transfer of income from one lot of rich people to another, a transfer in which the effects on the poor are small and incidental. Benefits to poor people are likely to be substantially less than if federal expenditure on equalization were targeted to the alleviation of poverty. There are not-completely-unrealistic circumstances where a program of equalization payments can be harmful on balance to the poor.

The bias against redistribution in a federation[5]

Over and above its direct impact on the revenues of the provinces, a program of equalization payments can exert an indirect influence on the distribution of income in the country as a whole by moderating the bias against redistribution in a federal system of government. There is, in any society, a basic conflict between the rich and the poor over the degree of redistribution, the rich typically wanting less and the poor typically wanting more. What is being called the bias against redistribution in a federal system of government is over and above that. Imagine a federal country where redistribution is conducted by the provinces exclusively, rather than by the nation as a whole, and consider a province within that country where the rich are politically dominant in decisions to tax and spend. The rich in such a province have a double incentive to limit the redistribution of income. Not only do they reduce the amount of tax they must pay to finance redistribution to the poor residents of their province, but stinginess on their part might reduce the number of recipients of redistribution by inducing some of the poor to migrate to other provinces where redistribution is more generous. A province has an incentive to establish itself as mean and ungenerous— emphasizing the virtue of self-reliance and self-sufficiency under the banner of "Live Free or Die"—to attract the rich and repel the poor. No province can afford to acquire a reputation for generosity for fear of attracting welfare recipients.

Much depends on the composition of public expenditure. The anti-redistributive bias in a federal system of government arises when, and only when, the out-migration from a province of a poor person conveys a net financial advantage to the remaining residents of the province and the out-migration of a rich person conveys a net financial disadvantage. That, in turn, depends on how total expenditure varies, for any given level of services, with the size and composition of the population of the province. At one extreme is the implicit assumption case (ii) in table II.3 that public expenditure is for a fixed requirement of a pure public good. If the $3,000 has to be spent regardless of how few or many people choose to live in a province, then the addition of an extra person, rich or poor, is always beneficial to the original residents as long as gross incomes are invariant (an assumption to be dropped below) and as long as that person pays any tax at all. Equivalently, if the required public expenditure increases together with population, but a poor person requires only a tenth of the public expenditure of a rich person—as might be the case if the only public expenditure were for a marina that was of no use to anybody who did not own a yacht—then inter-provincial migration would have no effect upon the non-migrant population, and the rich would have nothing to gain from the out-migration of the poor.

But if public expenditure is a fixed amount per head, rich or poor—as might be the case if expenditure were for province-wide public schooling—then the exodus of a poor person from a province is beneficial to those left behind, and the exodus of a rich person is harmful. Referring to the numbers in case (ii) of Table II.3, if public expenditure is fixed at $1,000 per head, then the exodus of the poor person, A3, from province A reduces required public expenditure from $3,000 to $2,000 and allows for a reduction in the provincial tax rate from 14.3 percent to 10 percent (2,000/20,000) with no loss of public services per head. Similarly, by lowering the tax base per head in province B, the migration of person A3 from province A to province B is harmful to everybody in province B, rich and poor alike. Required public expenditure increases from $3,000 to $4,000, the tax base increases from $12,000 to $13,000 and the provincial tax rate increases from 25 percent to 31 percent, (4,000/13,000). The anti-redistributive bias is even more pronounced when public expenditure per head is higher for the poor than for the rich—as when public expenditure is for welfare, public housing or services that the rich do not use at all.

When the required public expenditure within each province is more or less the same per person, the benefit to province A and the corresponding harm to province B from the migration of person A3 from province A to province B is moderated somewhat by equalization payments, but by no means eliminated. As computed above, the original entitlement of province B was $818, requiring a federal tax rate of 2.5 percent. With the migration of person A3 to province B, the national average provincial tax rate of 18.2 percent and the average provincial tax base per head of $5,500 remain as they were, but the tax base per head in province B falls from $4,000 to $3,250 (13,000/4), so that the required equalization payment to province B increases from $818 to $1,638 [.182(5,500-3,250)4]. The federal income tax to finance the new equalization payment rises from 2.5 percent to 5 percent (1,638/33,000) and the required provincial tax rate in province B is reduced from 31 percent to 18.2 percent [(4,000-1,638)/13,000], which is, as intended, the average provincial tax rate as it would be in the absence of the equalization program. The equalization payment preserves the provincial tax rate in the recipient province, but only by increasing the federal tax rate.

Without equalization payments, the net effect of the migration of person A3 to province B is to lower the provincial tax rate in province A from 14.3 percent to 10 percent, and to raise the provincial tax rate in province B from 25 percent to 31 percent. With equalization payments, the net effect of migration of person A3 to province B is to lower the total (federal and provincial) tax rate in province A from 16.3 percent (14.3 + 2.5) to 15 percent (10 + 5), and to raise the total (federal and provincial) tax rates in province B from 20.7 percent (18.2 + 2.5) to 23.2 percent (18.2 + 5). People in province B are better off than if there had been no equalization payments, but still worse off than if person A3 had not migrated at all. If the rich people, A1 and A2, in province A could somehow induce the poor person, A3, to depart, it would be still in their interest to do so. In particular, it would be in their interest to cut redistributive expenditures in the hope that person A3 might be induced to go. Nevertheless, within the context of this example, the argument that equalization payments serve to moderate the anti-redistributive bias would appear to be correct.

More generally, the argument is only half right. In a society with many provinces, it remains true that equalization payments dampen the redistributive bias within the recipient provinces. The in-migration of a poor person to a recipient province decreases its tax base per head but increases its entitlement to equalization payments so that revenue per head remains the same. Thus, the extent of redistribution in a recipient province can be chosen as though its population were invariant. Whatever determines the extent of redistribution when there is a fixed population would continue to do so in the presence of interprovincial migration. For a recipient province, the anti-redistributive bias associated with interprovincial migration of the poor would be mitigated to a very large extent.

That is not true of the donor provinces, or, to be more precise, such mitigation of the anti-redistributive bias as there may be is unlikely to be significant. The reason for the difference is that equalization payments are financed by federal taxation rather than by direct levies on the wealthier provinces. Suppose there were ten provinces rather than just two, five identical to province A and five identical to province B, and suppose that the one poor person Â3, in one of the rich provinces, Â, chooses to locate elsewhere. The effect of the out-migration of this person on the provincial tax rate in province Â, and on two rich people, Â1 and Â2, who remain there, is exactly as calculated above; the tax rate falls from 14.3 percent to 10 percent. But the effect on the federal tax rate is different. If the migrant goes to another rich province, there can be no effect on the federal tax rate at all because that province is not a recipient of equalization payments and the circumstances of the recipient provinces are unaffected. If the migrant goes to one of the recipient provinces, the federal tax rate to finance equalization payments would still increase, but the increase would be no more than a fifth of what it would be if there were two provinces rather ten. The increase in the entitlement to equalization payments of the province to which person Â3 goes would be as specified in the preceding paragraph, but, since the federal tax base is five times larger than before, the resulting increase in the federal tax rate would be just a fifth of what it was estimated to be. When there were just two provinces, the federal tax rate increased from 2.5 percent to 5 percent. When there are ten provinces, the federal tax rate increases from 2.5 percent to 3 percent. With ten provinces, the cost of the increase in the federal tax rate to finance the increase in equalization payments when a poor person migrates from a rich province to a poor province is borne for the most part by the other eight provinces, and the anti-redistributive bias is hardly moderated at all.

In moderating the anti-redistributive bias in poor provinces while leaving the bias more or less untouched in the rich provinces, a program of equalization payments has the entirely unintended effect of herding poor people into some provinces and concentrating the rich in others. Equalization payments are no substitute for nation-wide redistribution among people. Only nation-wide redistribution can eliminate the anti-redistributive bias by which generosity in any region of the country is self-defeating because it provokes the in-migration of the poor and the out-migration of the rich.

There is another consideration: though equalization payments moderate the incentive among recipient provinces to be ungenerous to the poor in the hope that the poor will go elsewhere, there is created no real incentive toward generosity. Equalization payments differ in this respect from federal grants to the provinces under the recently-abolished Canada Assistance Plan which matched provincial expenditure on welfare, dollar for dollar, so that a dollar contributed by a province to the poor entailed a net cost of only 50 cents. Equalization payments are cash grants to the recipient provinces which can do what they please with the money and are provided with no special incentive to devote the money to the alleviation of poverty. On receiving a dollar of equalization payments, the government of the recipient province acquires no greater incentive to increase its provision for the poor than it would acquire from an other increase in public revenue brought about by an increase in tax rates or by an exogenous expansion of the tax base.[6] Whatever may have induced the federal government in its 1995 Budget to abolish the Canada Assistance Plan while preserving the equalization program intact, it is hard to believe that the motive was to ensure that no citizen of Canada is second class, to share wealth, or to raise the income of the poor.

A mismatch between federal and provincial taxation

As transfers from the federal government to provincial governments, equalization payments must increase federal taxation and decrease provincial taxation for any given level of services. Thus the net effect of equalization payments on the distribution of income in Canada must depend in part on whether federal taxation is more progressive than provincial taxation. The benefit of equalization payments to the poor would surely be greater if federal taxation bears primarily on the rich and provincial taxation bears primarily on the poor than if federal taxation bears primarily on the poor and provincial taxation bears primarily on the rich. So far, this consideration has been overlooked in our examples where universal proportional income taxation has been assumed. And since the net effect of equalization payments upon the poor has so far been rather small, one might suppose that effect could be swamped by the mismatch in the degree of progressivity between federal and provincial taxation.

To illustrate this possibility, consider an example where provincial taxation is very much more progressive than federal taxation. Suppose all provincial revenue is raised by proportional income taxation, while all federal revenue is raised by a head tax. Except for this assumption, the example is the same as that in case (i) of table II.3.

The change in the assumption about the progressivity of federal taxation has no effect on entitlements to equalization, for these depend exclusively on provincial tax bases and provincial tax rates. Again, there is no equalization payment to province A and the total entitlement to province B is $818. In the example in table II.3, where federal revenue was raised by proportional income taxation, the federal tax rate was 2.48 percent, and the federal tax bill was $248 per rich person and $25 per poor person. Now, when federal revenue is raised by a head tax, the federal tax bill is $136 per person, rich or poor, and the net gains and losses from equalization payments are as shown in table II.4.

Under these assumptions, there is only one gainer from the program of equalization payments, the rich person in the poor province. Everybody else is a loser: the two rich people in the rich province because they must pay a share of the federal tax to finance the equalization payment to the poor province, the two poor people in the poor province because their gain of $68 (250 - 182), from the reduction in provincial tax made possible by equalization payments falls short of the $136 they must pay in federal tax to finance the program, and, especially, the poor person in the rich province whose total tax bill almost doubles because he must

Table II.4: The Financial Consequences of Equalization Payments with Proportional Income Taxation by the Provinces and a Head Tax by the Federal Government

People	Pre-Tax Income	Provincial Taxation with Equalization Payments	Provincial Taxation with Equalization Payments	Federal Tax to Finance Equalization Payments	Net Gain from Equalization Payments
A1	10,000	1,429	1,429	136	-136
A2	10,000	1,429	1,429	136	-136
A3	1,000	143	143	136	-136
B1	10,000	2,500	1,818	136	546
B2	1,000	250	182	136	-68
B3	1,000	250	182	136	-68
Total	33,000	6,000	5,183	818	0

pay his full share of federal taxation to finance equalization payments though his provincial tax bill is unchanged.

Of course, the major premise of this example may be false. All things considered, federal taxation may not be less progressive than provincial taxation. It is difficult to say with any degree of assurance whether the mix of federal taxes—personal income taxation with all of its loopholes and complications, corporation income taxation, the GST, tariffs, excise taxes and so on—is more or less favourable to the rich than the mix of provincial taxes. What can be said is that, when the tax system is complex and when the principal effect of equalization payments is to redistribute income among the rich, the net effect upon the poor is uncertain and unpredictable.

The opposite case is interesting. One might suppose that, if the combination of proportional income taxation by the provinces and a head tax by the federal government renders equalization payments especially harmful to the poor, then the opposite combination, proportional income taxation by the federal government and a head tax in the provinces, would render equalization payments especially beneficial to the poor. That turns out not to be so. The reason is that if provincial revenue were raised by a head tax, there would be no equalization payments at all! With a provincial head tax, the tax base in the equalization formula in equation I.1 would be people, the tax base per head would be the same for all provinces by definition, and each province's entitlement would be automatically equal to 0. Thus it is difficult to determine the relevance of the example in table II.4 for the assessment of the distributive implications of the Canadian program. If federal taxation is regressive, then there is a bias in equalization payments against the poor, but, if provincial taxation is regressive, the equalization payments themselves would be small.

A rich province may have a low tax base

The Canadian program of equalization payments rests upon an implicit analogy between the revenue of a province and the income of a person. A person is said to be rich when his income from all sources is large. For the assignment of equalization payments, a province is said to be rich when its income from all sources is large. The analogy may be harmless when income is the principal tax base of the provinces, but the analogy may be dangerously misleading when this is not so. When tax bases diverge substantially from income, a "poor" province might easily be composed of rich people, and an equalization payment to the "poor" province may turn out be a transfer from the poor to the rich. Governments, federal and provincial, have many tax bases, the different bases are taxed at different rates and the distribution among provinces of particular tax bases need not correspond to the distributions among provinces of income per head. For instance, a province with a larger than average resource base per head, a smaller than average endowment of physical or human capital per head and, on balance, a lower than average income per head might not be entitled to equalization payments if provincial tax rates were significantly higher on resource-based income than on income from other sources.

The perverse case where poor people live in rich provinces may be illustrated for a country with two industries and two provinces, where populations in the two provinces are the same, people's endowments are identical within each province, but endowments per head in the two provinces are different. The industries are α and β. Province A is predominant in industry α, province B is predominant in industry β and income per head is larger in province A than in province B. Specifically, each person in A earns $50,000 from industry α, and $20,000 from industry β for a total of $70,000, while each person in province B earns $20,000 from industry α and $30,000 from industry β for a total of $50,000. Province A is unambiguously rich relative to province B; every single person in province A is better off than every single person in province B. If all federal and provincial revenue were raised by proportional income taxation, a program of equalization payments would provide a net transfer money from province A to province B and, in doing so, would constitute a net transfer from rich people to poor people in the country as a whole.

All this may change if income originating in the different industries is not taxed at the same rate. Suppose each province requires a public expenditure of $10,000 per head, that there is no tax on income originating in industry α and that, never mind why, all federal and provincial revenue is raised by proportional taxation of income originating in industry β exclusively. There may be something about industry α that makes it difficult to tax. Perhaps it is easier to evade tax on income from industry α than to evade tax on income from industry β, so that the full social cost of taxation would be substantially larger per dollar of revenue on industry α than per dollar of revenue on industry β. Regardless, to finance provincial public expenditure of $10,000 per head with a tax on industry β, province A (with a tax base of $20,000 per head) must impose a tax rate of 50 percent, while province B (with a tax base of $30,000 per head) can get by with a tax rate of 33⅓ percent. Thus, Province A counts as the have-not province in the Canadian equalization formula even though it is, in reality, the richer province and the net transfer under the program would be from poor people to rich people.

Since the average provincial tax rate is 40 percent (20,000/50,00) and the average tax base is $25,000 per head, the required equalization payment to province A is $2,000 per head [.4(25,000 - 20,000)]. To raise that money with a nation-wide tax on income from industry β, the federal tax rate would have to be 4 percent, (2,000/50,000), yielding $800 per head from province A and $1,200 per head from province B. Thus, the net effect of the program of equalization payments is to increase the income per head in province A by $1,200 (2,000 - 800), and to decrease the income per head in province B accordingly, a net transfer of $1,200 per head from poor people in province B to rich people in province A.

Again, this example is an extreme one, chosen to illustrate a phenomenon cleanly. The significance of the example is that the effects of equalization payments become increasingly ambiguous and difficult to trace as provincial tax systems diverge from pure income taxation. Provincial tax revenues—from income taxation of people and corporations, sales taxes, property taxes, license fees, income of public corporations, and so on—do not line up neatly, one to one, with the components of the personal income of the typical resident of the province. The Canadian program of equalization payments is less likely to narrow the gap between rich and poor in Canada as a whole the greater the divergence of the tax structures in the provinces from pure income taxation, the greater the differences among provincial tax structures, and the greater the divergence between tax structure of the federal government and the tax structures of the provinces.

Mobility, incidence and equalization

The story changes substantially when we allow for inter-provincial mobility of labour and other factors of production. A key assumption so far has been that the gross, pre-tax, and pre-transfer income of every person in the economy is invariant. Thus, for example, the incomes of persons A1, A2, and A3 in table II.3 are what they are (specifically $10,000, $10,000, and $1,000) regardless of the behaviour of governments. Net incomes change in response to changes in taxation and public expenditure, but gross incomes remain the same. The assumption is plausible enough as long as people cannot migrate from one province to another, but it creates a distorted picture of the effects of equalization on the economy if, and to the extent that, migration is possible. In so far as equalization payments, and federal taxation to finance equalization payments, tend to augment or reduce the net incomes of the *immobile* factors of production, the story in table II.3 is quite satisfactory. In so far as the incomes of *mobile* factors of production are affected, a new set of considerations comes into play.

To see what is involved here, imagine an economy where output in both provinces is produced with land and labour, where the essential characteristic of land is its immobility and where the essential characteristic of labour is its capacity to move costlessly from one province to another. Also suppose for convenience that people are either workers who supply labour but own no land, or landlords who do not work, and that landlords must live on their land to collect the rent. All workers are equally productive and equally well off. Within each province, all landowners have equal amounts of land and collect equal amounts of rent. Thus, in a two province economy, there are three classes of people: landowners in province A, landowners in province B and workers who might live in either province. Though people within each class are equally well off, we need not specify in advance which class is poor, which is rich, and which is in between. Unrealistic as it is, the sharp distinction between land and labour is useful for classifying people's response to taxation and transfers, and to draw out the implications of the responses of people with different endowments for the distribution of income in the country as a whole.

For landowners in either province, "money sticks where it hits." A transfer of income to landowners in province A is beneficial to landowners in province A, and to nobody else. A tax on landowners in province A reduces their incomes, but leaves unchanged the incomes of landowners in province B and of all workers. The same, with the appropriate change of labels, is true of landowners in province B. There is no shifting.

Labour is entirely different. A transfer to (or tax on) labour in one province is automatically shifted to all labour in both provinces together, and the incomes of landowners in both provinces are significantly affected. Ignoring for the moment how federal funds are acquired, it can be said that a transfer by the federal government to workers in province B alone *raises* the incomes of workers in both provinces, *raises* the incomes of landowners in province B and *lowers* the incomes of landowners in province A.

The mechanism is this: Prior to the transfer, the net incomes (after taxes and public services) of workers in both provinces are the same. Were that not so, workers would have migrated from the province where their net incomes are low to the province where their net incomes are high, driving up wages in the former province where labour has become more scarce and driving down wages in the latter province where labour has become more plentiful, until wages in both provinces are equalized. Initially, the transfer to workers in province B increases their net income and opens a gap between the net incomes in province B and province A. The gap in the wages induces workers to migrate from province A to province B until wages are the same once again. The common post-tax and post-transfer income is necessarily higher than before, but less than net income in province B alone would have been if the transfer-induced migration had not taken place.

As mobility of labour equalizes net labour income in both provinces, the relation between wages paid by employers in the two provinces and the transfer per head in province B is specified in equation II.1

$$\begin{pmatrix} \textit{Wage Paid} \\ \textit{per Worker} \\ \textit{in Province A} \end{pmatrix} = \begin{pmatrix} \textit{Wage Paid} \\ \textit{per Worker} \\ \textit{in Province B} \end{pmatrix} + \begin{pmatrix} \textit{Transfer} \\ \textit{per Worker} \\ \textit{in Province B} \end{pmatrix} \qquad \text{(II.1)}$$

The increase in the number of workers in province B must lead to an increase in the incomes of landowners in that province because the wage that landowners must pay workers (recall that the net income of a worker in province B is the sum of the wage paid by landowners and the transfer) is lower than before. The gain to landowners in province B is at the expense of landowners in province A who must now pay higher wages and whose rents are necessarily reduced by the transfer-induced exodus of labour.

Finally, consider the impact of federal taxation to finance the transfer. Federal funds can be acquired by the taxation of land or of labour. If, and in so far as the transfer is financed by a land tax, then the gain to labour is preserved. A proportional tax on all rents imposes an additional burden on land in province A, and introduces a burden on land in province B, a burden that may or may not outweigh the gain from the transfer-induced migration. If, however, the transfer is financed by a tax on labour in both provinces, then the initial gain to all labour may but need not be wiped out. All things considered, there is a net gain to labour if the sensitivity of the wage to the supply of labour is greater in province B than in province A.

It is customary and convenient to represent sensitivity of wages to labour supply by an "elasticity," defined as the percentage by which the wage rate falls in response to a given percentage increase in the availability of labour. Thus, for example, to say, as I shall, that the elasticity of wage to labour supply is -½ in province A, is to say that competition among landowners and workers in province A leads to a ½ percent fall in the going wage when the number of workers in the provinces increases by 1 percent. This elasticity describes not the behaviour of workers, but the response of the market to a change in the number of workers seeking employment. The elasticity is negative because one variable goes down as the other goes up.

To nail down the connection between equalization payments and the net wage of labour in both provinces, it is convenient as an intermediate step to consider a slightly different mechanism. Consider a transfer to labour in province B financed by federal taxation of all labour everywhere. This mechanism would be the same as equalization payments if all land were exempt from tax. For such a mechanism, it is to be shown how the common net wage of labour may rise or fall with the introduction of equalization payments depending on conditions of production in the two provinces as reflected in the sensitivities of wages to labour supply.

The combined effect of the transfer to workers in province B financed by a tax on all workers in both provinces is illustrated in table II.5. The numbers in the table are based on an internally-consistent model of the labour markets in the two provinces.[7] The table shows that the common net income of labour is increased if and only if conditions of production in the two provinces are such that the wage of labour is less sensitive to the supply of labour in the recipient province than in the other province. Specifically, the demand for labour in each province is assumed to be such that, in the absence of the transfer, a total labour

Table II.5: Transfer to Labour in Province B Financed by a Tax on Labour in Both Provinces (Total Labour Force is 200)

Province	Number of Workers	Total Income of Province ($)	Rent of Land ($)	Wages Paid by Employers ($)	Net Income per Worker (After Transfer but Before Tax) ($)	Net Income per Worker (After Transfer and Tax) ($)
Case (i) Elasticity of wages with respect to labour force is -1/2 in Province A and -3/4 in Province B without transfer					
A	100	10,000	5,000	50	50	50
B	100	20,000	15,000	50	50	50
With transfer of $1000 to workers in Province B					
A	86	9,274	4,637	53.9	53.9	48.9
B	114	20,665	15,501	45.3	53.9	48.9

Percentage Gain (+) or Loss (-)   %

to land in Province A   -9.3

to land in Province B   +3.3

to labour   -2.2

to National Income   -0.2

Table II.5 (continued)

Province	Number of Workers	Total Income of Province ($)	Rent of Land ($)	Wages Paid by Employers ($)	Net Income per Worker (After Transfer but Before Tax) ($)	Net Income per Worker (After Transfer and Tax) ($)
Case (ii) elasticity of wages with respect to labour force is -1/2 in Province A and -1/4 in Province B without transfer						
A	100	10,000	5,000	50	50	50
B	100	6,667	1,667	50	50	50
With Transfer of $1000 to Workers in Province B						
A	80	9,944	4,472	55.9	55.9	50.9
B	120	7,643	1,919	47.7	55.9	50.9
Percentage Gain (+) or Loss (-)				%		
to land in Province A				-10.5		
to land in Province B				+15.1		
to labour				+1.8		
to National Income				- 0.5		

force of 200 workers would be allocated equally between the provinces and the common, market-clearing wage would be $50 per worker in both provinces. Then, to illustrate how the effects of a transfer depend on assumptions about the elasticity of the wage rate to the availability of labour, we imagine a transfer a transfer of $1,000 from the federal government to workers in province B, financed by a tax of $5 per head on workers in both provinces. If labour were not mobile, there would be a net gain of $5 to each worker in province B (a transfer of $10 coupled with a tax of $5), a net loss to each worker in province A of $5 and no change in rents in either province. As labour is mobile, net wages have to be equalized.

Two cases are compared. In both cases, the conditions of production in province A are chosen so that the elasticity of the wage rate with respect to labour supply in province A is -½; a 1 percent increase in the supply of labour causes a ½ percent decrease in the wage. In the first case, the corresponding elasticity in province B is -¾, signifying that wages are more sensitive to labour supply in province B than in province A. In the second case, the corresponding elasticity in province B is -¼, signifying that wages are less sensitive to labour supply in province B than in province A. In both cases, the transfer of income to workers in province B draws workers from province A to province B until net incomes in the two provinces are once again the same, but the size of the migration required depends on the elasticities of wages to labour supply.

In case (i), where the wage rate is more sensitive to labour supply in province B than in province A, the transfer induces 14 out of 100 workers in province A to migrate to province B, raising the rent of land in province B by 3.3 percent, lowering the rent of land in province A by 9.3 percent, increasing the wage of labour in province A from $50 to $53.9, decreasing the wage of labour in province B from $50 to $45.3 and *decreasing* the common net income of labour (wage plus transfer less the federal tax of $5 per worker tax to finance the transfer) by 2.2 percent from $50 to $48.9. In case (ii), where the wage rate is relatively sensitive to labour supply in province A, the transfer induces a larger reallocation of labour between the provinces, a more pronounced effect on the rents of land, and an *increase* in the common net income of labour of 1.8

percent from $50 to $50.9. Though the tax and subsidy are levied on labour alone, their primary impacts are on rents rather than wages, and their net impact on the income of labour can be up or down depending on the magnitudes of elasticities that are in practice difficult if not impossible to measure. Note finally that, in both cases, there is a tiny reduction of the national income of the country as a whole; its significance will be discussed under the heading of efficiency below.

The impact of a program of equalization payments on the distribution of income can be especially perverse when labour is mobile and income differentials are attributable to skill rather than to the ownership of land. Ignore land (and capital) altogether, and consider an example with two provinces, two goods and two skill groups. Suppose i) each good can be produced in one province only, good A in province A and good B in province B, ii) the relative price of the good A in terms of good B depends on amounts produced, which in turn depends on the number and average skill of workers in province, iii) everybody is equally skilled at producing good B, but skilled workers are *twice* as productive as unskilled workers in producing good A, iv) there are few enough skilled workers that *all* skilled workers and *some* unskilled workers are in province A producing good A, while the rest of the unskilled workers are in province B producing good B, and finally v) in each province, a fixed overhead cost of administration is financed by a proportional income tax on all workers in the province.

It is evident what happens. As long as there is enough demand for the good A to employ both types of workers (i.e. some unskilled workers and all skilled workers) in province A, the net after-tax wage of skilled workers must be twice that of unskilled workers and the net after-tax wages of unskilled workers must be the same in both provinces. Goods prices adjust to ensure that this is so. Thus, net income per head in A with some skilled workers and some unskilled workers must exceed income per head in province B with no skilled workers at all.

Under the Canadian formula, an equalization payment is warranted to province B, so that the tax rate is lowered in province B and a federal tax is imposed on all workers to finance the equalization payment. The initial effect of the equalization payment is to raise the net incomes of unskilled workers in province B above their net incomes in province A, driving some unskilled workers from province A to province B, lowering the output of good A, increasing the output of good B and raising the relative price of good A until net incomes of unskilled workers are the same once again. The equalization payment cannot be equalizing among people because relative wages of skilled and unskilled workers remain as before in province A. The gap between wages of skilled and unskilled workers could be narrowed by federal progressive income taxation or by targeted transfers to poor people wherever they reside, but equalization payments will not do.

What does this tell us about equalization payments? More than anything, it muddies the waters, indicating that, in general, the incidence of equalization payments is highly uncertain and that the ultimate beneficiaries of a program of equalization payments may not be those for whom the program was intended. In particular, one should be aware of the heroism in the assumption that the entire range of factors of production can be represented by the simple dichotomy between completely mobile labour and completely immobile land.

These considerations should be born in mind: first, labour as a factor of production may be mobile, though many workers are not. For labour to be mobile, it is sufficient that enough workers be prepared to move between provinces to equalize net incomes. It does not matter if most workers are a bunch of old sticks-in-the-mud who would never leave their provinces in any circumstances. The key assumption is substitutability between those who go and those who stay. Second, substitutability is always a matter of degree. Every worker has some person-specific local knowledge that must go to waste when he migrates. Third, the real basis of the distinction between land and labour in the example is the attachment, or lack of attachment, of people to the resources they own. People can always move from one place to another. Their skills must accompany them, but their land and capital need not. Fourth, even non-human resources are mobile to some extent. Machines can be can often be shipped from one place to another. Factories that cannot literally be moved from one place to another are mobile in time, as depreciation in one location is covered by new investment in another. Land itself is mobile to some extent in this sense of the term. All factors of production are mobile at a cost which may be relatively low for skills and relatively high for land. Fifth, there is no necessary connection between land, as the term is used here, and wealth. "Land" may include the meagre dwellings of the poor as well the mansions, factories, oil wells and gold mines of the rich. "Labour" may include highly skilled workers who are relatively rich. Capital, which is formally ignored in table II.5, may be quite mobile, and therefore more like labour than land. The example in table II.5 establishes that equalization payments tend to favour owners of immobile factors, whoever they may be, in the recipient provinces and to harm owners of immobile factors in the other provinces. It also shows that the effects on mobile factors of production are in practice unpredictable. But who in practice is mobile is often very difficult to say.

Thus in some complex and ill-specified way, the net effect of equalization payments on the income distribution in the country as a whole is a composite of the stories in tables II.1, II.3, and table II.5. The simple story in table II.1 may be relevant to Newfoundland where people are significantly worse off than in the rest of Canada, but it is almost irrelevant to Quebec where the standard of living is much closer to the national average and where there are significant numbers of very wealthy people. Among the main beneficiaries of equalization payments are the taxpayers in the recipient provinces, in proportion to the amounts of tax they pay, and the owners of the immobile factors of production in the recipient provinces who may, but certainly need not, be rich. Even that is uncertain, for the ultimate effect of a program of equalization payments on the welfare of citizens depends critically on patterns of taxation and expenditure in the provinces and the federal government, and on how these patterns change in response to the program. It depends on the degree of progressivity in the federal and provincial tax structures, on the composition of their tax bases and on the strength of the bias against redistribution, with and without equalization payments. Whether, on balance, the equalization program constitutes a net transfer to the poor in the country as a whole is distinctly problematic. But ignorance is itself a kind of knowledge when the unthinking presumption in public discussion, a presumption with little basis but the common usage of words, is that equalization payments must, of course, be equalizing.

Equalization payments may improve the lot of the very poor in the very poorest provinces, but whatever degree of equalization of incomes among Canadians is obtained in a program of equalization payments could, almost certainly, be obtained at a fraction of the cost to the federal government by direct transfers to the poor. There are better routes to equality. The approximately $8 billion that the federal government spends on equalization payments would be more than sufficient to provide a $500 cheque for every man, woman and child in Canada, as long as the money was taxable so that prosperous Canadians would automatically return half the sum in extra tax payments. That would almost certainly be more equalizing than equalization payments are today. Other ways of spending, or of reducing federal taxes, by $8 billion are better still. The Canadian program of equalization payments cannot be justified as an instrument for the promotion of equality of income among all Canadians. Other considerations must be invoked if equalization payments are to be justified at all.

Part III: Efficiency

EFFICIENCY IS THE ABSENCE OF WASTE. An economy is efficient when resources are employed and goods are allocated among people to make everybody as well off as he can be, in the special sense that no redeployment of resources and no reallocation of goods among people can make anybody better off without harming somebody else. Broadly speaking, and subject to qualifications that will not be discussed just yet, an economy is efficient when its national income is maximized. Broadly speaking, a program of equalization payments is efficient if it raises the national income above what it would otherwise be. There are many ways for a program of equalization payments to influence the efficiency of the economy, raising or lowering the national income as the case may be. The examination of the efficiency of equalization payments in this chapter will place the effects of the program into five categories: the allocation among the provinces of labour and other factors of production, the social cost of taxation, the amount and composition of public expenditure, and two lesser considerations, insurance against province-wide misfortune and the administrative cost of an equalization program. These will be examined in turn.

The allocation among provinces of labour and other mobile factors of production[8]

Unequal resource revenue

Turn back to table II.5. The table is intended to illustrate the effects on the distribution of income among workers, landowners in province A, and landowners in province B, of a transfer of income to workers in province B financed by a tax on workers in the country as a whole. The lesson in the table is that these effects are uncertain because they extend well beyond the immediate beneficiaries of the transfer. Only workers are subsidized or taxed, but the big winners and the big losers are not workers at all. The immediate impact of the transfer is to raise net incomes of workers in province B and lower net incomes of workers in province A, opening a gap between the net incomes of workers in the two provinces. Then, the transfer-induced migration of workers from province A to province B restores the equality between their net incomes, and, in doing so, raises rents in province B and lowers rents in province A by larger percentages than the change in the net income of workers. Whether the overall distribution of income becomes wider or narrower depends primarily on which landowners are initially prosperous. One might expect the distribution of income to widen if landowners in province A are relatively poor and to narrow if landowners in province A are relatively rich. There is another effect. In equalizing net incomes of workers, the transfer-induced migration of labour necessarily generates a discrepancy between the marginal products of labour in the two provinces, and, in doing so, reduces the national income to some extent. Regardless of whether the net income of workers is increased or decreased, the combined value of output in the two provinces together is somewhat less than in the absence of the transfer and the tax to pay for it. As a consequence of the transfer, the combined income in the two provinces falls by 0.2 percent from $30,000 to $29,939 (9,247 + 20,665) in case (i) and by 0.5 percent from $16,667 to $16,587 (8,944 + 7643) in case (ii). In both cases, the transfer is inefficient, though the proportion of national income lost is very small.

The transfer in a program of equalization payments is in some respects like the transfer to labour in table II.5. People in some provinces are subsidized by people in all provinces through the intermediary of the federal government. The transfers would be identical if the response of the governments of the recipient provinces were to reduce the tax burden on labour alone, and if federal taxation were confined to labour. The transfers differ in their impact on the economy to the extent that these conditions do not hold. Nevertheless, on the strength of this common feature, one might be inclined to surmise that the inefficiency story in table II.5 might extend to equalization payments as well. One would not always be wrong in reasoning so, but it is commonly believed, with some justification, that the effect of equalization on the national income is in the other direction, that equalization payments promote, rather than detract from, efficiency in the allocation of resources among the provinces. The reason is that equalization payments are only supplied in circumstances where there is already a distortion in the economy and where equalization payments serve as a corrective. This possibility is illustrated in table III.1, which is an extension of table II.5.

Table III.1 shows the impact of equalization payments on the national income of a country with two provinces and two sources of income: wheat produced in both provinces with land and labour, and resource revenue from, let us say, oil that gushes all by itself from the ground ready for use or sale. The example in table III.1 extends the example in table II.5 by adding a second commodity with special characteristics. Though commodities were not identified in table II.5, there is no harm in supposing that both provinces grow wheat, and that the price of wheat is $1 per bushel, so that the dollar value of income and the production of wheat in bushels are one and the same. On that assumption, table III.1 is an extension of case (i) of table II.5. The top slices of the two tables—describing the economy as it would be without resource revenue and without equalization payments—are identical.

Table III.1: The Impact of Equalization Payments on the Size and Distribution of the National Income when One Province has Resource Revenue

Province	Number of Workers	Output of Wheat $	Income of Landowners $		Wage of Labour $	
			Rent of Land	After Transfers and Taxes	Paid by Employers	After Transfers and Taxes
Without resource revenue or equalization payments						
A	100	10,000	5,000	5,000	50	50
B	100	20,000	15,000	15,000	50	50
Total	200	30,000	20,000	20,000	—	—
With oil revenue of $4,000 in Province A but without equalization payments						
A	125	11,180	5,590	7,368	45	62
B	75	18,612	13,959	13,959	62	62
Total	200	29,792	19,549	21,327	—	—
With oil revenue of $4,000 in Province A, an equalization payment of $2,492 to Province B and Federal income taxation to finance the equalization payment						
A	118	10,863	5,432	6,840	46	60
B	82	19,032	14,274	14,988	58	60
Total	200	29,895	19,706	21,828	—	—

Effects of $2,492 of equalization payments
(i) National income increases by $103 or 0.3%
(ii) Net income per worker decreases by 3.3%
(iii) Net income of landowners in Province A decreases by $528 or 7.2%
(iv) Net income of landowners in Province B increases by $1029 or 7.4%.

The key assumption in table III.1 is that resource revenue belongs to province A alone. To focus clearly on the efficiency of equalization payments, the technology of wheat production in the two provinces is exactly as in case (i) of table II.5, and the numbers of landowners in the two provinces are chosen so that, in the absence of resource revenue and with costless mobility of labour, every single person's income would be the same. The total population in both provinces together is 600, of whom 200 are workers who are free to locate in either province, 100 are landowners in province A and 300 are landowners in province B. As in table II.5, the equilibrium allocation of labour places 100 workers in each province. In these conditions, everybody's income is exactly $50, or, equivalently, 50 bushels of wheat.

In the middle slice, the technology of wheat production remains unchanged, but there is assumed to be $4,000 of oil revenue in province A alone. Oil revenue accrues in the first instance to the government of province A which redistributes it in equal amounts to each and every person in the province. Enough workers then move from province B to province A and, accordingly, there is a sufficient increase in the wage paid to workers in province B and a sufficient decrease in the wage paid to workers in province A that, when the workers' share of the oil revenue in province A is taken into account, the net incomes of workers in the two provinces are equalized once again. The equilibrium allocation of workers to province A rises from 100 to 125, and, as there are 200 workers in total, the allocation of workers to province B falls to 75. Labour is uninvolved in the production of oil, but the allocation of labour between the provinces is affected regardless. As in the example in table II.5, the returns to land are affected significantly.

One might suppose that the introduction of $4,000 of oil revenue would raise the total national income from $30,000, as it was in the absence oil revenues, to $34,000. That is not quite what happens. The concentration of oil revenue in one province leads to a misallocation of labour. Workers move to province A not because they are more productive there, but as the only means of acquiring a share of the oil revenue. Thus, as can be seen in the second slice of table III.1, the total output of wheat falls from $30,000 to $29,792, and there is a waste, a deadweight loss, of $208 which is the amount by which national income would be larger if the allocation of the labour force remained as it was before the introduction of the oil revenue. Note particularly that the inefficiency in this example is a direct consequence of the rule in province A for distributing the oil revenue. There would be no misallocation of labour and no inefficiency if the oil revenue were restricted to landowners in the province or to a fixed group of people who could claim to be the original residents of the province. The inefficiency arises because and only because anybody who chooses to reside in province A can claim a share.[9]

The equalization program reverses the process to some extent. To avoid a multitude of problems while preserving the essence of the situation, ignore ordinary public expenditure and suppose that the only activity of the provincial governments is to distribute the oil revenue and the transfer, if any, from the federal government. On this assumption, and in the absence of a program of equalization payments, the government of province B is dormant, and the sole activity of the government of province A is to distribute oil revenue equally among the 100 landowners and the 125 workers who choose to reside in the province. When a program of equalization payments is introduced in accordance with equations I.3 and I.4, the federal government transfers $2,492 to the government of province B, which would then share that amount equally among all residents of the province. (Since there is no provincial tax revenue in province B and since public ownership of oil revenue is the equivalent of a tax rate of 100 percent, the appropriate payment by the federal government to province B is the provincial tax base per head (4,000/600) in the country as a whole multiplied by the population of province B (375).) The rate of federal income taxation to finance the payment to province B turns out to be 8.3 percent.

The outcome when oil revenue in province A triggers an equalization payment from the federal government to the government of province B is shown in the bottom slice of table III.1. Now there are two fiscal influences upon the allocation of labour between the provinces: the initial provision to each worker in province A of a share in the oil revenue, and the provision in province B of a share of the province's equalization payment. But fiscal influences do not cancel out. The rules of the equalization program guarantee that a share of the oil revenue is worth more than a share of the equalization payment, so that more workers remain in province A than if there had been no oil revenue at all. As shown in the top slice of the table, the labour force in province A would be 100 had there been no oil revenue and, therefore, no equalization payment. As shown in the middle slice, it increases to 125 with the introduction of oil revenue. As shown in the bottom slice, it falls to 118 when oil revenue gives rise to equalization payments. The output of wheat changes accordingly, falling by $208 from $30,000 to $29,792 with the appearance of oil revenue, and then rising again by $103 to $29,895 with the introduction of equalization payments. The equalization payment generates an increase in the national income, but the inefficiency from the unequal distribution of oil revenue is not reversed altogether.

Several questions are suggested by this example: a) How general is the efficiency gain from equalization payments? Is it limited to the maldistribution of ownership of oil revenues or is there a wide range of inefficiencies in the federal government that may be moderated by equalization payments? b) How large is the gain in efficiency likely to be? In the example, an equalization payment of $2,493 led to an increase in the national income of $103, which is less than five percent of the transfer. Is there reason to believe that the Canadian program of equalization payments does significantly better than that? c) Are there forces working in the opposite direction, so that the gain itself may, in practice, be illusory?

Natural resources, public goods, shared goods, and the redistribution of income

The source of the inefficiency in table III.1 is that the initial allocation of the oil revenue is to one province exclusively. There would be no misallocation of labour between the provinces if the oil revenue had accrued in the first instance to the nation as a whole, so that one could benefit equally from the oil revenue regardless of where one lived. Nor would there have been a misallocation of labour if the oil were privately owned and not subject to taxation. Everything depended on where jurisdiction was assigned, but the assumption about jurisdiction was not unrealistic.

Section 92A(4) of the Canadian Constitution provides the provinces with jurisdiction over natural resources, including the authority to

> make laws in relation to the raising of money or any mode or system of taxation in respect of a) non-renewable natural resources and forestry resources in the province and the primary production there from, and b) sites and facilities in the province for the generation of electrical energy and the production there from

The value of jurisdiction over natural resources is enhanced considerably by Section 125 protecting provincial resource revenue from taxation by the federal government:

> No Lands or Property belonging to Canada or any Province shall be Liable to Taxation

And, exactly as in the example, nature has endowed some provinces with considerably more than their share.

A disparity in resource revenue among the provinces induces a misallocation of labour, causing the national income in the country as a whole to be less than it would otherwise be. The crux of the matter is that competition among workers and employers in the market for labour sets wages equal to the worker's contribution to the national income, that is, to his marginal product of labour. If wages exceeded (or fell short of) the worker's contribution to output, then employers would hire fewer (or more) workers until the equality is restored.

Without the resource revenue, wages in any two provinces would be the same. If resource revenue were suddenly to appear in one province only and if all workers remained where they were before, there would immediately emerge a gap between incomes of labour (wages plus the transfer to the worker or the reduction in provincial income tax made possible by provincial access to resource revenue) in the two provinces. The presence of the gap would induce inter-provincial migration, because migrants from one province to another automatically acquire shares of the resource revenue in the provinces to which they come, and lose their shares of the resource revenue in the provinces from which they go. As the work force in the resource-rich province increases, the marginal contribution of labour to output in that province must fall and the wage must fall accordingly until the gap between workers' incomes is closed. The closing of the revenue-induced gap between the net incomes of labour in the two provinces leads to the opening of a migration-induced gap between the contributions to output of labour and other mobile factors of production.

Provincial ownership of natural resources is not the only source within the public sector of misallocation of labour among the provinces. A similar misallocation may arise when public goods or overhead costs are financed by provincial taxation where "public" in this context means that the benefit or advantage to each and every person in the province is independent of the population of the province. A public good is an item, such as a television signal, that conveys its full benefit to everybody within range, regardless of how many or how few people make use of it. A public overhead cost, such as the cost of the provincial legislature, conveys no direct benefit to the citizen but is required for the province to function at all. On coming to a province and paying tax there, a migrant automatically conveys a net benefit to all of the original residents of the province by assuming a share of the overhead cost and the cost of public goods in the province. In so far as provincial expenditure is on public goods and overhead cost, any difference between the tax the migrant must pay in the province from which he comes, and the tax he must pay in the province to which he goes, is analogous to the acquisition of a share of provincial resource revenue, and generates a similar misallocation of labour. Once again, equalization payments to provinces with low tax bases per head would rectify the situation to some extent.

There is some question about the significance of this consideration because the bulk of provincial government expenditure is not accurately characterized as provision of public goods or public overhead cost. A distinction can usefully be drawn between public goods and what might be called "shared goods." Shared goods are like public goods and unlike private goods in that the benefit of any given amount is the same for each person in the province, but they are like private goods and unlike public goods in that the cost per unit of benefit to each person increases directly with the number of people in the province. A shared good might be useful for its own sake, or it might be in the nature of an overhead cost. Public education is a shared good in so far as every child is educated equally. The police force is a shared good, or, more exactly, a shared overhead cost, in so far as the total cost of any degree of police protection rises in proportion to the total population, so that the cost per head remains the same.

The reason for emphasizing this distinction is that there need be no counterpart for shared goods of the inefficiency arising from differences among provinces in genuine overhead cost or need for public goods. Of course, provinces may differ in the cost per head of shared goods, but that need not induce a misallocation of labour. Suppose shared goods with the same benefit per head cost $1,000 per head in province A and $500 per head in province B, and suppose provincial taxes vary accordingly. In that event, the equilibrium money wage and the marginal product of labour must be $500 larger in province A, but there is no inefficiency because the migration of one person from province B to province A imposes an additional overhead cost of $500 on the economy as a whole. Differences among provinces in the cost of shared goods are unlikely to be very large except, perhaps, in the far north, where distance imposes costs of its own.

A misallocation may arise from the implicit sharing of income among the residents of a province when provincial revenue is acquired by proportional or progressive taxation. Provincial taxation at a rate t is comparable to provincial ownership of a fraction t of the income of the province. When a person pays, say, $10,000 in provincial tax, that $10,000 belongs, in the first instance, to the government of the province and ultimately to the people of the province for whom it is the equivalent in every respect to $10,000 of resource revenue. Thus, the richer the province, the greater the public revenue for any given rate of provincial taxation, and the more attractive the province to a prospective immigrant. A person drawn to a province to acquire a share of oil revenue would be equally drawn if, instead, a given level of public services could be financed at a low provincial tax rate (or a high level of public services could be financed at a given provincial tax rate) because the average income in the province is high. Whether provinces differ in resource revenue or taxable income, the misallocation of labour from fiscally-induced migration is the same. This inefficiency is magnified when provinces engage in explicit or implicit redistribution of income. With federal jurisdiction over the redistribution of income, a person becomes eligible for benefits in accordance with his income and (though there are some exceptions in Canada) regardless where he chooses to reside. With provincial jurisdiction, and as long as rich provinces are not significantly less generous than poor provinces, potential beneficiaries are drawn to especially rich or especially generous provinces until compensatory gaps emerge between the wages of identically-skilled people in different provinces.

Consider once again the six person example in table II.2 where each province is assumed to have an overhead cost of $1,000 per person and where public revenue is acquired by income taxation. The gap between the income tax rates in the two provinces—25 percent in province B and 14.3 percent in province A—when there are no equalization payments, is like resource revenue in province A that is shared among residents in accordance with their incomes, a bonus in province A of 10.7 percent of one's income, whatever that happens to be. The lower tax rate in province A draws people from province B just as surely as if province A had oil revenue to redistribute. The consequences for the allocation among provinces of the mobile factors of production and for the rents of land in the two provinces are exactly the same. The role of equalization payments is the same too. A program of equalization payments moderates the inefficiency in interprovincial allocation of resources by compensating province B for the financial advantages in province A and reducing the gap between provincial tax rates for any given level of public services.

A program of equalization payments may be efficient when provincially-owned natural resources are distributed unequally, or when provinces require different overhead costs or supply different amounts of public goods per head (though this is not true of shared goods), or when tax rates are lower in rich provinces than in poor provinces because fixed public expenditure per head is financed by proportional taxation, or when provincial governments differ in the amount of redistribution they provide. In all of these conditions, there is a presumption that a program of equalization payments *may* raise the national income somewhat. That, however, is not a decisive argument for efficiency in practice. The argument is that equalization payments would be efficient in certain conditions. There remains doubt about whether these conditions obtain. There remains reason to fear that the gain may be small or illusory.

First, as already discussed under the heading of equality, the corrective supplied by equalization payments is almost certain to be incomplete. Second, there is, to my knowledge, no empirical evidence that the gain is substantial, while the weight of argument and such evidence as there is suggests that the gain, if any, is very small indeed. It is certainly small in the example in the example in table III.1. The gain there is $103 out of a total equalization payment of $2,492, a ratio of 1 to 25. Were that the true proportion of the gain from the reallocation of labour, then the actual gain from the $8 billion of payments in the Canadian program would be $335 million, an amount that could easily be swamped by other considerations described below. In fact, the only empirical estimate of that ratio is not 1 in 25, but 1 in 500![10] Third, the major premise in the argument that equalization payments correct a preexisting misallocation of labour may turn out to be false. As will be explained below, equalization payments might easily work in the wrong direction, exaggerating a distortion rather than reducing it. The simple presumption from table II.5 that a transfer by the federal government to selected provinces is *per se* inefficient may turn out to be correct after all. Distortions generated by differences among provinces in resource revenue or by province-wide redistribution may be swamped by the effects of other social programs that tend to inhibit the out migration of people from poor provinces. Fourth, equalization payments may generate costs or benefits over and above their effects on labour and other factors of production.

The context of equalization payments

Equalization payments were shown to be efficient within the context of the example in table III.1 by improving the allocation of labour between the provinces, by drawing the actual allocation of labour toward the allocation that maximizes the national income as a whole. The magnitude of the improvement is small, but the direction is unambiguous. There is some question as to whether the example is indicative of Canadian conditions. The central assumption in the demonstration of the efficiency of equalization payments is that they are only supplied when there would otherwise be too few people in the recipient province and too many people elsewhere. In the Canadian context, there would have to be too *few* people in Newfoundland and Prince Edward Island and too *many* people in Alberta and British Columbia. The lesson in the example would seem to be that equalization payments enlarge the national income of Canada by inhibiting the emigration from poor provinces to rich provinces. Efficiency is alleged to consist of inducing people in the "have not" provinces, who might otherwise migrate to the "have" provinces, to remain where they are. That does not conform to most people's sense of what is good for the Canadian economy.

The nub of the problem is the assumptions in the construction of the example that a) the maldistribution of resource revenues is the only distortion in the economy, and b) the program of equalization payments is the only public policy affecting the allocation of the national labour force. By contrast, if the national labour force were misallocated initially—with too many workers in province B and too few workers in province A—for some other reason, then a maldistribution of resource revenues, such as is assumed in the example, could serve as a *corrective* for the misallocation of labour, and equalization payments could easily *reduce* the national income in the country as a whole. That may be exactly what is happening in Canada. There may be too large a proportion of the Canadian labour force in Newfoundland because the provision of welfare and unemployment insurance induce people to stay or because labour is less mobile than is assumed in the example. In these conditions, equalization payments may be inefficient by providing workers in Newfoundland with an extra reason not to seek opportunities elsewhere.

To put the argument in the usual language of formal public finance, it may be said that equalization payments are not necessarily efficient in their impact on the allocation of labour and other mobile factors of production because equalization payments are not necessarily restricted to provinces where the "net fiscal benefits" (a term to be defined presently) are small.[11]

Consider a person deciding whether to migrate from province B to province A. His decision to migrate would be "efficient" if the national income is increased, that is, if that person's contribution to the national income on migrating to province A exceeds his contribution by remaining in province B. As a worker's contribution to the national income is automatically reflected in his wage, the net gain to society when a worker moves from province B to province A is just the difference between the wages in the two provinces.

$$G_S = w_A - w_B \qquad\qquad\qquad\qquad\qquad\qquad (\text{III.1})$$

where G_S is the net gain to society (or loss if G_S is negative), w_A is the wage in province A, w_B is the wage in province B, and it is understood in interpreting the equation that w_A and w_B are for comparable skills, for two doctors or for two day labourers in different provinces, not for a doctor in one province and for a day labourer in another. As long as G_S is positive, the national income can be increased by the migration of a worker from province B to province A. Consequently, the national income is as large as it can be, and the allocation of labour is efficient, when $G_S = 0$. (The extra cost to a province of providing public services for one extra person is being ignored. This simplification can easily be modified without changing the essence of the story.)

The potential migrant sees matters differently. He migrates if it is in his interest to do so. Of course, he looks at the difference in wages between the two provinces, but he also takes account of taxes and public services. Province A, for example, would be the more attractive province if wages and public services were the same as in province B but taxes were lower. The potential migrant chooses between provinces to obtain the larger value of the sum of his wage and his "net fiscal benefit," where one's net fiscal benefit is the value of all public services received (inclusive of transfer payments) less one's tax bill. Net fiscal benefit is large when resource revenue enables a province to keep taxes low, to provide desirable public goods, or to offer a large transfer of income through welfare or unemployment insurance. Obviously, net fiscal benefits need not be the same for everybody in a province; they may be high for the poor and low for the rich, or vice versa. But in this context, there is no harm in supposing that all potential migrants are alike.

By contrast with gain to society in equation III.1, the gain to the individual is

$$G_I = (w_A + N_A) - (w_B + N_B) \tag{III.2}$$

where N_A and N_B are the net fiscal benefits in the two provinces. Since workers are assumed to be mobile, and since one migrates from province B to province A whenever $G_I > 0$, the allocation of the labour force can only be in "equilibrium" when $G_I = 0$.

Thus, the allocation of labour is optimal when there is no longer any social gain to migration, that is where $G_S = 0$, while the market equilibrium allocation of labour is where there is no longer any private gain to migration, that is where $G_I = 0$. Specifically, if the net fiscal benefit in province A were higher than that in province B, then the wage in province A would have to be lower, and the allocation of labour would be inefficient on that account. (If $N_A > N_B$, then $G_S > 0$ whenever $G_I = 0$.) That is the case where equalization payments may be helpful.

Equalization payments could be unhelpful if $w_A > w_B$ but $N_B > N_A$, as might be the case if equalization payments are provided to provinces where out-migration is inhibited by welfare or unemployment insurance. Equalization payments could also be unhelpful when labour markets are not in equilibrium. If $G_I > 0$ but workers in province B are a bunch of old sticks-in-the-mud with a preference for remaining where they are, and who require a premium to overcome their reluctance to migrate, then the introduction of a program of equalization payments can depress the national income by deterring the migration that would otherwise occur.

There is another consideration. Sections 92A(4) and Section 125 of the Canadian constitution place resource revenues in the hands of the provinces and shield these revenues from federal taxation. Presumably the wise Canadian statesmen who placed these clauses in the Canadian constitution were not completely unaware of their allocative and distributive consequences. The assignment of resource revenues to the provinces was the assignment of income to particular groups of people. But those same wise Canadian statesmen also opted for Section 36(2) which takes a considerable amount of that income away, removing with the left hand what was granted with the right. In evaluating the impact of equalization payments on the disposition of resource revenue and the effects of that disposition on the inter-provincial allocation of mobile factors of production, one must make up one's mind about the ownership of natural resources. One must make up one's mind about the entitlement to the fruit as well as the formal ownership of the tree. If the public's share of natural resource revenue is to be divided equally among all Canadians, then natural resources should be under federal rather than provincial jurisdiction. If the public's share of natural resource revenue is to be reserved for residents of the province where the resource is located, then provincial ownership would seem to be warranted and equalization payments would be undesirable. If the public's share is to belong to the people of the province where the resource is located subject to the restriction that income from resource revenue be taxed like private income by the federal government for the benefit of all Canadians (that owners of income from natural resources should contribute to the running of the federal government as do owners of all other sources of income), then Section 125 might be revoked but the present equalization program would be the equivalent of confiscatory taxation.

The full cost of tax collection

Why the cost of raising revenue might be higher for poor provinces than for rich provinces

We have been reasoning so far as though the only consideration in the assessment of the efficiency of a program of equalization payments is the loss of output from the misallocation among provinces of labour and other mobile factors of production. That is an important consideration, but it is not the only one. Equally if not more important is the effect of a program of equalization payments on the full cost of public revenue in the nation as a whole.

Taxation is always doubly costly to the taxpayer. There is a cost of the tax he pays and a cost of the tax he avoids paying. The tax he pays conveys a benefit to the rest of society by providing the resources to finance the government. The tax he avoids paying conveys no benefit to the rest of society, but is costly to the taxpayer all the same. It is costly because real resources are used up or real benefits forgone in the attempt to deflect liability for tax. Real resources wasted in the diversion from activities that are relatively productive but taxed to activities that are relatively unproductive but untaxed: from labour to leisure, from high taxed to low taxed goods, from investment to consumption, from sale to barter, from employment to do-it-yourself and from above-ground to underground transactions. In these diversions, each dollar gained by the tax avoider is matched by a dollar lost to others whose taxes must be increased to cover the cost of public expenditures, so that the expenditure of time and effort in tax avoidance is a waste, "excess burden" or "deadweight loss" of taxation to society as a whole.

Consider a person choosing how many hours to work. He picks a number of hours such that his benefit from the income earned in the last hour of work is just equal to his benefit from the hour of leisure he would have enjoyed instead. This must be so, for he would have worked more if the income were preferred to the leisure, and he would have worked less if the leisure were preferred to the income. Without income taxation, his choice would be of no concern to the rest of society because the value of what he buys with his wage would be equal to the value of what he produces to earn it. Income taxation has two effects in this context. On the one hand, it opens a gap between the value of what one can buy with one's wage and the value of what one produces to earn it, a gap consisting of the benefit to the rest of society from the tax one pays. On the other hand, it induces the taxpayer to shift from work to leisure by reducing the net, after-tax income from one's wage without at the same time affecting the value of leisure. Together these effects of income taxation impose a cost on the rest of society, for the potential tax revenue from the extra hours one would have worked but for the tax is, in a sense, wasted.

A similar story can be told about the purchase of a commodity on which an excise tax is imposed. Let the retail price of a commodity be $20 per pound, of which $15 is the cost of production and $5 is provincial sales tax. At a price of $20, each person in the province buys 100 pounds of the commodity from outlets where the provincial sales tax is collected. Now suppose that the provincial sales tax is raised by $1 per pound, that there is a corresponding increase in the retail price within the province from $20 to $21 per pound and that each person responds to the rise in price by reducing his purchase within the province from 100 pounds to 90 pounds. He may purchase less of the commodity or he may buy more out of province. Had the amount purchased remained the same, the revenue to the province would have increased by $100. Since the amount purchased falls, the extra revenue is only $40, the difference between the original revenue of $500 (5 x 100) and the new revenue of $540 (6 x 90).

But the burden of the tax increase to the consumer is about $100 all the same. This is because he bears an extra dollar of tax on each pound he buys within the province at the new tax-inclusive price of $21, together with an extra dollar of cost on every $21 he diverts from the purchase of the taxed commodity to other activities—more leisure, utilization of sources of supply out of province, hiding income from the tax collector, or diversion of expenditure to less taxed commodities. When the tax was only $5 a pound, he was prepared to spend up to $5 to hide the purchase of one pound from the tax collector, and he took advantage of every opportunity to do so. Now that the tax has risen to $6, he is prepared to spend up to $6 to hide the purchase of a pound from the tax collector. He spends the extra dollar per pound regardless of whether he pays the tax or not. A 5 percent rise in the tax rate imposes a cost of $100 on the taxpayer, of which $40 is public revenue and the remaining $60 is deadweight loss, a waste to the province though there may be some effect on the amount of revenue raised in neighbouring jurisdictions. That must be so, for otherwise the taxpayer would not purchase the amount he does or would not divert purchasing power to the extent that he does to other activities. Thus, each dollar of extra provincial revenue imposes a burden of $2.50 (100/40) on the taxpayers in the province.[12]

Though this example is made up, the phenomenon it represents is genuine enough, and has a distinct bearing on federal-provincial financial relations. Several aspects of deadweight loss are important for the assessment of the efficiency of a program of equalization payments. First, the deadweight loss per dollar of tax revenue may be considerably greater for some taxes than for others, depending on the ease with which tax can be avoided. The deadweight loss is likely to be rather small for land taxes because the tax base is what it is regardless of how large a tax is imposed. The deadweight loss is likely to be larger for income taxation because the taxpayer can make all or part of his taxable income disappear by working less, diverting effort to do-it-yourself activities, barter, or outright tax evasion. The higher the tax rate the greater the incentive to engage in such stratagems.

Second, regardless of how tax is avoided, and regardless of whether the avoidance is legal or illegal, the cost of avoidance to society is an increasing function of the rate of taxation, negligible at low rates, substantial at high rates. When tax rates are low, only the inexpensive ways of converting taxable income into untaxed benefits would be worthwhile for the taxpayer because, at a high cost of avoidance, it would be cheaper to pay the tax. But as tax rates increase, more and more expensive diversions become advantageous. In the example, a 5 percent rise in the tax rate generated a burden of $2.50 per dollar of revenue. Had the tax rate been smaller, the extra cost of taxation would have also been smaller too, and the burden on the taxpayer per unit of revenue might have been close to one. Had the tax rate been higher, the extra cost of taxation would have exceeded $2.50 per dollar of revenue.

Third, there is usually a top rate beyond which an increase in the rate leads to a decrease in tax revenue, though the burden to the taxpayer remains high. Cigarette taxes are sometimes set above the top rate because they are designed not just to raise revenue, but to deter smoking. No government would knowingly exceed the top rate if the sole object of taxation were to raise revenue.

Fourth, for any given amount of public revenue, the mix of taxes should be chosen to minimize the total deadweight loss in the country as a whole. That, in turn, is achieved when the additional deadweight loss per dollar of additional tax revenue from a slight increase in the tax rate is the same for each and every tax base. If, at existing tax rates, it costs $3 to raise a dollar of revenue by increasing the excise tax but only $2 to raise an extra dollar of revenue by increasing the income tax, then, ideally, the excise tax should be lowered and the income tax raised accordingly.

Fifth, the deadweight loss in taxation may be larger for the provinces than for the federal government because there is often more scope for avoiding provincial tax than for avoiding federal tax. For example, any tax on labour, federal or provincial, can be avoided to some extent by working less, but a provincial tax on labour can also be avoided by moving to another province. When income from labour is taxed in both of two provinces, A and B, an increase in the tax rate in province A must drive some workers from province A to province B, increasing provincial revenue in province B for any given rate of tax, and reducing tax revenue in province A accordingly. That the loss of revenue to province A is in part matched by a gain in revenue to province B is no consolation to the taxpayers of province A, who must bear the cost regardless. By contrast, a nation-wide tax on labour income would have no comparable effect, except in so far as labour is internationally mobile. Similarly, an increase in the tax on gasoline in province A induces some residents in province A to purchase gasoline in province B instead, raising tax revenue in province B, lowering tax revenue in province A and, since the effect is symmetric, deterring both provinces from taxing gasoline to some extent. This is probably why it is the practice in most federations for the central government to collect more revenue than is required to finance the services it provides and to pass the extra revenue down to lower levels of governments. The difference in excess burden between the federal government and the provinces may be the real reason for the EPF (Established Program Financing) and its successor the CST (Canada Social Transfer) in which the federal government transfers revenue to all of the provincial governments.

Together, these considerations amount to an argument for equalization payments if and only if there is reason to believe that the total cost of taxation per dollar of revenue would otherwise be higher in poor provinces than in rich provinces. There would be no such case for equalization payments if the cost were uniformly higher for the provinces than for the federal government or if tax rates in the absence of equalization payments would be more or less the same among provinces, as they might be if people, rich or poor, wanted their provincial governments to spend the same *proportion* of provincial gross domestic product. A case for equalization payments may emerge when all provincial governments spend approximately the same *amount* per person, regardless of whether the province is rich or poor.[13]

Provinces might require equal spending per person to maintain national standards in some public services. If, to take the most important example, the federal government seeks to maintain national standards of publicly-provided medical care, and if medical care remains under the jurisdiction of the provinces, then the provincial tax rate to finance medical care would have to be higher in poor provinces than in rich provinces, unless the federal government provides poor provinces with enough revenue to keep rates the same. In the extreme, transfers from the federal government may be absolutely necessary for a poor province to maintain national standards because it may be literally impossible to do so otherwise. It is conceivable that a province could not supply the average public services in the country as a whole with the tax base at its disposal. It is conceivable that revenue would remain insufficient even when tax rates are raised to the point where additional increases would prove self-defeating because the tax base would shrink by more than the tax rate is increased. Though this "doomsday scenario" is rather unlikely for any Canadian province, a program of equalization payments might remove a considerable part of the excess burden in provincial taxation. The rationale for supplying equalization payments on actual tax bases, rather than on, say, provincial gross domestic product per head, might be to subsidize provinces that would otherwise bear an especially large social cost of taxation.

The argument is plausible but by no means decisive. Though equalization payments allow recipient provinces to engage in national average expenditure at national average tax rates, they do not require the provinces to do so. Recipient provinces may use the revenue from equalization payments to reduce taxes instead and may provide no public services over and above what would be provided in the absence of equalization payments. If the maintenance of national standards for certain public services is driving the equalization program, it might be preferable for the federal government to finance these services completely in all provinces or to provide these services itself. More will be said about this presently. Equalization payments are a lump sum transfer to certain provinces, and, as such, provide the provinces with no particular incentive to spend on this rather than on that, or to use the extra revenue to increase public expenditure at all.

Nor do we know the full social cost of all of the different modes of taxation that the provinces may choose to employ. We do not know when the social cost of taxation is large and when it is small. We do not know to what extent the tax structure of the provinces is chosen to minimize the full social cost per dollar of tax revenue, and to what extent it is chosen for other reasons. We have no basis for supposing that the Canadian equalization formula comes at all close to what would be required to minimize the full social cost of taxation. As tax bases vary considerably from one province to another, we cannot be certain that the "have not" provinces would be compelled to impose taxes with large excess burdens if equalization payments were not forthcoming. We have no real assurance that the allocation of federal money among the provinces, in so far as the tax bases of the province diverge from income per capita, is anything but frivolous and random.

Equalization payments might distort the incentive of the provinces to raise revenue efficiently[14]

The mix of taxes in each province and the set of transfers from the federal government to the provinces are conducive to nation-wide efficiency if and only if the total deadweight loss of the federal and provincial tax system is minimized, and that, in turn, is only attained by equalizing the full cost of an additional dollar of revenue of each and every tax. In the absence of equalization payments, it would be in the interest of each and every province to minimize the total deadweight loss of its own tax system by equalizing the full cost of an additional dollar of revenue from each and every tax base in that province. A program of equalization payments would be inefficient if and in so far as it provoked provinces to depart from that ideal. A program of equalization payments may do just that because the formula allows provinces to influence the magnitudes of their transfers under the program by adjustments in their tax rates.

A program of equalization payments would be neutral—neither efficient nor inefficient—in its effects on the total expenditure and tax structure of the provincial governments if the amounts transferred under the program were seen by the provinces as invariant, as fixed sums of money that are what they are regardless of what the provinces choose to do. The program ceases to be neutral when provinces recognize that their entitlements under the program are larger or smaller depending on how they behave. The program becomes inefficient when provincial expenditure and taxation are slanted to augment transfers from the federal government. Three inefficiencies may be introduced. Provinces receiving equalization payments have an incentive to overspend, and other provinces have an incentive to underspend. All provinces have an incentive to levy high rates of tax on their deficit bases. All provinces have an incentive to hide tax bases. These matters will be discussed in turn.

The incentive of recipient provinces to overspend is evident from the simplified equalization formula in equation III.3 for an economy where all public revenue, federal and provincial alike, is raised by income taxation. The entitlement of province B is

$$E_B = t_C(y_C - y_B)P_B \qquad \qquad \text{(III.3)}$$

where P_B is the population in province B, y_B is the income per head in province B, y_C is average income per head in the country as a whole and t_C is the average provincial tax rate. It is immediately evident that the government of province B can raise an extra dollar of public revenue by something less than an extra dollar of taxation on the residents of the province because an increase in the provincial tax rate leads to an increase in the average provincial tax rate in the country as a whole and to a corresponding increase in the province's entitlement to equalization payments.

Suppose, in a country with two provinces, that province A is relatively rich with an income per head of $100,000, province B is relatively poor with an income per head of $50,000, the provinces have equal populations, all provincial revenue is raised by income taxation and, initially, the tax rate is 10 percent in both provinces. The average income per head is $75,000 and the average provincial tax rate is 10 percent. Provincial revenue per head is $10,000 in province A and $5,000 in province B. When equalization payments are provided in accordance with equation III.3 above, the federal government must provide province B with a payment of $2,500 per head [(0.1)(75,000 - 50,000)]. Total public revenue per head in province B rises to $7,500 of which $5,000 is tax revenue and $2,500 is the equalization payment. The federal income tax rate to finance the program of equalization payments must be 1.667 percent [2,500/(100,000 + 50,000)], and the federal tax bill per head is $1,667 [(.01667)(100,000)] in province A and $833, [(.01667)(50,000)], in province B. The net gain per head in province B is $1,667, which is the difference between the equalization payment of $2,500 per head and the province's share, $833 per head, of the federal income tax to pay for it.

Now suppose province B raises an additional $2,000 per head of public revenue by increasing its provincial tax rate from 10 percent to 14 percent. The average provincial tax rate, t, rises to from 10 percent to 11.33 percent, [(10,000 + 7,000)/(100,000 + 50,000)], the required equalization payment automatically rises to $2,833, [(.1133)(75,000—50,000)], per head and the rate of the federal income tax to finance program rises to from 1.667 percent to 1.889 percent, [(2,833)/(100,000 + 50,000)]. By raising its tax rate, province B acquires extra revenue from two sources, the taxation of its own residents and the equalization payments of the federal government. Altogether, the net increase in the revenue per person in province B is $2,333, [2,000 + 2,833 - 2,500], while the net increase in the federal and provincial tax bill per person in province B only is $2,111 [2000 + (.01889 - .01667)50,000], the increase in provincial tax plus the province's share of the increase in federal tax to finance the increase in equalization payments to province B.

Residents in province B pay 90 cents on the dollar for additional public expenditure, [2,111/2,333]. Ten cents out of every dollar is paid by the residents of province A whose federal income tax bill must rise to finance the extra equalization payment. Since equalization payments reduce the cost of public services in recipient provinces, an incentive is created in recipient provinces to rely more on the public sector and less on the market. This consideration could be important when public services are a close substitute for private goods. There is a similar incentive for provinces that do not receive equalization payments to cut back on provincial public expenditure, lowering t_C in the equalization formula in equation (III.3) and reducing their federal tax bill.[15]

A second perverse incentive on provincial governments arises when there is more than one provincial tax base so that a given amount of expenditure can be financed with high taxes on some bases and low taxes on others, for example, with high income taxes and low property taxes, or vice versa. The perverse incentive derives from the possibility of influencing equalization payments by adjusting the mix of provincial tax rates. Every province acquires an incentive to impose high taxes on deficit bases and low taxes on surplus bases. With two tax bases, the Canadian equalization formula of equation I.4 becomes

$$E_i = \textit{the larger of } [0,\ t_{C1}(Q_{C1} - Q_{i1})P_i + t_{C2}(Q_{C2} - Q_{i2})P_i] \qquad \text{(III.4)}$$

where the tax bases are identified as 1 and 2, i refers to a province, C refers to the country as a whole, E refers to an equalization payment, t refers to a provincial tax rate, Q refers to a tax base per head and P refers to the population of a province. Suppose that province i is among the provinces entitled to equalization payments, that base 1 is a deficit base for province i and that base 2 is a surplus base for province i. Base 1 is a deficit base for province i when the term $(Q_{C1} - Q_{i1})$ is positive, signifying that the province i has less than its share of the first tax base. Base 2 is a surplus base for province i when the term $(Q_{C2} - Q_{i2})$ is negative, signifying that the province i has more than its share of the second tax base. It is immediately evident from an inspection of equation III.4 that the province can increase its entitlement to equalization payments without increasing the amount of tax it collects by increasing its rate on base 1 and decreasing its rate on tax base 2 accordingly, so that net revenue from the two taxes together remains the same. This manoeuvre increases the province's entitlement to equalization payments by influencing the average provincial tax rates, t_{C1} and t_{C2}, raising the weight in the formula of the deficit base, and lowering the weight of the surplus base.

The gain from this ploy depends critically on the extent to which a province's tax rate on any particular base affects the average provincial tax rate on that base in the country as a whole. Typically, a small province would have a small influence on average provincial tax rates, but that is not universally so. The province of Prince Edward Island would have almost no leverage over the average provincial income tax rate, but it would have every incentive to avoid a special excise tax on the production of potatoes because it would lose almost a dollar's worth of equalization payment for every dollar collected from such a tax. If province i is Prince Edward Island, if production of potatoes is base 1 and if average production per head in the rest of Canada is negligible, (so that Q_{C1} is approximately zero and t_{C1} is approximately equal to the rate of excise taxation on the production of potatoes in Prince Edward Island), then a decrease in the excise tax on potatoes decreases $t_{i1} Q_{i1}$ in equation III.4, increasing E_i by the full amount of the tax and lowering the burden on the taxpayers of Prince Edward Island with virtually no loss of revenue to the province. Similarly, though the province of Alberta is not a recipient of equalization payments, the government of Alberta can reduce the burden of federal taxation on the residents of Alberta by lowering its tax on petroleum and raising other taxes accordingly to maintain provincial revenue. Tax ploys by the provinces can be harmful to the nation as a whole by increasing the social overhead cost of provincial taxation and by intensifying the conflict among provinces for federal largesse. Each province gains from the increase in its entitlement to equalization payments or from the decrease in the amount of federal tax its residents must pay to finance the entire equalization program, but each province's gain is at the expense of other provinces in a process that leaves national income of Canada somewhat lower than it would otherwise be.

All taxation is costly, in that the full burden to the taxpayer exceeds the amount of revenue collected. All taxation involves a social overhead cost in tax collection, in diversion of resources by the private sector from higher taxed but more productive activities to lower taxed but less productive activities, and in the wastage of effort in tax evasion and tax avoidance. For every province, there is an optimal mix of tax rates on the different provincial tax bases, a mix such that all Canadians are as well off as they can be for any given amount of public expenditure. A program of equalization payments distorts each province's choice of tax rates because the province's entitlement is dependent to some extent on its tax structure. The prospect of gaining or losing equalization payments induces a province to choose a mix of tax rates that is optimal for itself, but no longer optimal for the nation as a whole, for a province takes no account of the cost to the rest of Canada of the equalization payments it receives. The resulting inefficiency is similar in kind, though more difficult to quantify, to the inefficiency when mobile resources are misallocated among provinces as a consequence of differences in provincial tax rates. Both depress the national income to some extent.

The third perverse incentive upon provincial governments is to hide their tax bases or to take no action when residents of the province choose to do so. If, referring to the simple formula in equation III.3, the true tax base of the recipient province B is y_B but the province can somehow pretend that the tax base is only y_{B^*} (where $y_{B^*} < y_B$), then the equalization payment is increased by $t_C (y_B - y_{B^*})$ where t_C is the average provincial tax rate. If, in addition, the provincial tax rate in province B is the same as the average provincial tax rate in the country as a whole, then the ploy reduces tax payments by the residents of province B without sacrificing provincial revenue at all! For any given provincial tax rate, there is a slight loss of provincial revenue if the rate in province B is higher than average, and a slight gain if it is lower than average. Otherwise, provincial tax not paid within the province is automatically made up by federal transfers that are ultimately financed by taxpayers in the country as a whole. Residents of the province gain at the expense of residents in the rest of the country. Similarly, it is of little concern to the ordinary taxpayer if his fellow citizens in the province cook the books to convey the impression that their incomes are small, for the loss of provincial revenue is automatically made up by a federal transfer under the equalization program. The other side of that coin is that a province receiving equalization payments may have little incentive to invest in revenue-producing enterprises because the province's entitlement is reduced, in some cases dollar-for-dollar, when the revenue accrues. There is not much point in investing today if the return is to be equalized across provinces tomorrow.

A program of equalization payments supplies provincial governments with opportunities for setting tax and expenditure policies to draw revenue directly from the federal government and indirectly from the residents of other provinces. In aggregate, these manoeuvres are self-defeating, for the national income shrinks as each government strives to maximize its share in a classic prisoner's dilemma where self-interested ploys by all parties make everybody worse off than if other, more accommodating policies had been adopted. Knowing that entitlement to equalization payments is affected by the behaviour of provincial governments, the provinces and the federal government must surely bargain over what that behaviour will be. Such bargaining is undoubtedly unpleasant, and may well generate animosity as each party threatens the others with dire consequences if its point of view is not "understood." Strategic tax-setting, financial rivalry among the provinces, and manoeuvring for federal transfers tends to weaken the bonds that hold the country together, a matter to be discussed under the heading of equity below.

The composition of public expenditure

It has so far been shown that a program of equalization payments can influence the efficiency of the economy in the allocation among the provinces of mobile factors of production and in the mix of taxes that the provinces choose to levy. The working definition of efficiency was the maximization of the national income. It was argued that the test for the maximization of the national income is the equalization among provinces of the contributions of each factor of production and the equalization among taxes of the cost of an extra dollar of revenue. It was shown that efficiency was promoted by equalization payments imperfectly, if at all. Now a third aspect of efficiency is introduced, the effects of a program of equalization payments on the size and composition of provincial expenditure. This will be discussed under three headings: spillovers in provincial expenditure, the maintenance of national standards, and equal provision of public services.

To discuss these matters effectively, one must appeal to a larger concept of efficiency than the maximization of the national income. Efficiency in this context becomes the absence of waste in the broad sense that there is no further scope in the economy for making anybody better off, except at the expense of somebody else. If people in my town want signposts painted red, if people in your town want signposts painted blue, and if there is no confusion in having different coloured signposts in different places, it is efficient in this broader sense that both groups get their way, even though the colouring of the signposts has no effect on the national income as commonly defined. Thus, governments can be said to act efficiently when the right boundary is established between the public and private sectors and when the right mix of public services is chosen, regardless of whether the national income, narrowly defined, is increased.

Spillovers in provincial public expenditure

Provincial expenditures have consequences beyond the borders of the province. A road in province A is used by people in province B. Education of children and provision of medical care in province A conveys benefits to province B because well-educated and healthy people have high earnings and pay high taxes to the federal government and because, as some residents of province A will migrate to province B, it is better for the original residents of province B that the newcomers be well educated. Universities in all provinces accept students from across the country.

From the interdependence among provinces—expenditures in one province conveying benefits to another—it is sometimes argued that expenditure in the "have not" provinces should be promoted, so that expenditures per head in all provinces can be more or less the same, but the chain of reasoning to a rationale for equalization payments is long and treacherous. The natural policy implication of spillovers in provincial expenditure is the subsidization of all provincial expenditure, not equalization payments. If a dollar of educational expenditure in any province conveys 50 cents of benefits to the rest of the country, then the right inducement for educational expenditure is a dollar-for-dollar matching grant from the federal government, so that all provinces spend more on education than they would otherwise be inclined to do. Equalization payments are inappropriate on two counts. They are not provided to rich provinces which may be as prone to underspend as poor provinces, and they are provided to each province as a lump sum, regardless of the amount or composition of provincial expenditure. (Provinces can influence their entitlements to equalization payments through their mix of taxes but not through their mix of expenditures.) Thus, equalization payments provide no inducement to concentrate provincial expenditure on items that convey benefits to the rest of the country, nor any significant incentive to increase provincial public expenditure at all, except in so far as the provinces might be inclined to devote part of any increase in wealth to the purchase of extra public services.

National standards and local specificity

It is commonly believed that some goods should be supplied to everybody equally, regardless of where they live and regardless of whether they are rich or poor. Medical care, when provided by the public sector, is the prime example. To say that national standards are desirable is to say that local preferences "ought" to be overruled, as might be the case if different coloured signposts in different places would confuse motorists and cause accidents. Concern for national standards, though not universal among Canadians, is reflected in the Canada Health Act, which entitles the federal government to penalize any province that fails to adhere to national standards of provision. The question at issue here is whether national standards for the provision of some goods adds a new dimension to the argument for equalization payments on grounds of efficiency.

Suppose national standards are mandated for medical care. In principle, national standards can be established i) by federal provision of medical care, ii) by provincial provision with federally-imposed standards and federal funding, or iii) by provincial provision with federally-imposed standards but without federal funding. In the first two of these three options, there is no call for equalization payments because national standards place no burden on the provincial governments. Only in the third might there be a role for equalization payments because uniform expenditure per person requires high tax rates in poor provinces and because high tax rates entail large excess burdens, as discussed above, or to compensate poor provinces for spending more on medical care than they would be prepared to spend voluntarily in the absence of national standards.

It might be asked why services for which there are national standards should be provided by the provincial governments at all. Would it not be preferable to supply such services by the federal government to obtain national standards automatically? A common answer to this question is that each provincial government meets national standards in its own way, in accordance with the tastes and character of the people in the province. The argument is that provincial provision of services is efficient because it respects local specificity, while equalization payments correct for the alleged inequality or inefficiency that arises when given expenditures require different tax rates in different provinces.

The argument is questionable at best, for, except in Quebec, local specificity may not be characteristic of provinces at all. Ignore Quebec for the moment. Consider just the English-speaking provinces, and ask why, if expenditure in some category of public services is to be the same across provinces, it is not preferable for those services to be supplied uniformly by the federal government. How exactly might local preferences differ from one province to another so as to warrant provincial jurisdiction when national standards are to be maintained? Is there an intrinsic Manitoban, as distinct from an Ontarian, manner of delivery of medical care? Are the lungs and livers of the people of Manitoba different enough from the lungs and the livers of the people of Ontario to warrant separate jurisdiction over medical care? What is it that little children in Manitoba learn at schools under the jurisdiction of the province of Manitoba, or little children in Ontario learn at schools under the jurisdiction of the province of Ontario, that they could not all learn at schools under the jurisdiction of the federal government? Or is the local specificity argument a cover for governments seeking to preserve the domains of their authority?

Provinces are not towns. It is understandable that one might want to run local government locally, that the Kingston police force or the local clinic should be responsible to the Kingston City Council. But the Ministry of Health in Toronto is just as remote from the City of Kingston as a Ministry of Health in Ottawa would be. The division of powers under the Canadian constitution may be no more than an anachronism from a time before the introduction of air travel and the fax machine.

Quebec is the exception because language is an inextricable part of all delivery of public services. No doubt the government of the province of Quebec is as jealous of its authority as any other provincial government, but there is, in addition, a concern on the part of the majority of the people of Quebec that services be delivered in French, and a belief that French is best preserved by provincial jurisdiction. Outside of Quebec, language has no bearing on the relative advantages of federal and provincial jurisdiction. There are, of course, specific communities—the Metis, the Dukhobors, racial minorities and native people—whose preferences for public services may differ in some respects from the preferences of the majority of Canadians, but these communities tend to be minorities in their provinces as well as in Canada as a whole, and there is little basis for supposing that their interests are better looked after by the provinces than by the federal government.

In any case, the local specificity argument is an argument for federalism, not for equalization payments. Only if it can be shown that federalism requires equalization payments, or works very much better with a program of equalization payments, does local specificity have any bearing on the question of whether equalization payments are desirable.

Whether equal provision is desirable

National standards aside, it is often claimed—a proposition almost implicit in the wording of Section 36(2)—that public expenditure "should" be the same per person in every province, though the composition of that expenditure is best left to the discretion of provincial governments. The word "should" in this context has a double meaning. It may be an instrumental should on a criterion of equality or efficiency, or it may be a moral should in which case other considerations would have to be introduced. This chapter is concerned with efficiency exclusively. Other considerations are introduced in the next chapter.

Over and above the effects of equalization payments on the allocation of labour among provinces and the cost of raising revenues, there is sometimes alleged to be a virtue in equal provincial expenditure for its own sake. It is thought desirable for the provinces *to be able* to provide equal values of services per head at equal rates of tax, regardless of whether they *actually* provide equal services or not. One way of describing this virtue is to say that equalization payments provide (or would do if equalization were down as well as up) a federal system of government with the financial equivalent of a unitary state, such as France or the U.K. In an ideal unitary state, the same mix of services would be provided at the same tax rates everywhere, though some municipal independence would presumably be allowed, as it is today in virtually every country in the world. In a federal system of government with equalization payments, the mix of services would differ among provinces but the total value of services need not.

The Canadian equalization program does not obligate provincial governments to maintain the same expenditure per head or the same mix or value of public services. Nor is it likely that the provinces will do so voluntarily. Provinces may prefer to preserve the same *proportion* of government expenditure to gross domestic product, rather than to preserve the same *dollar value* expenditure per head. Just as rich people and poor people prefer to spend different amounts of money on housing (though they might spend the same proportions of their incomes), so might rich and poor provinces prefer to spend different amounts on the services provided by their provincial governments. Given sufficient funds to provide equal public services per head, poor provinces might prefer to divert much of those funds to consumption of private goods. Nor, except where national standards are involved, is there any particular virtue in equal provincial expenditure per head.

Right or wrong, Canada allows large disparities of income among people. Some Canadians are very wealthy; others are very poor. There is no particular reason why the same should not also be true of provinces. Indeed, we should be less solicitous of provinces than of people, because people are our primary concern. In saying this, I am not retracting any of the arguments for or against equalization payments elsewhere in this book. I am merely asserting that there is no additional case for equalization payments in the proposition that the composition of public output can be improved.

Equalization as insurance

A program of equalization payments might be justified as interprovincial insurance. Provinces that are prosperous today provide assistance through the intermediary of the federal government to provinces that are poor today, in the expectation that they in turn will be assisted if they become poor tomorrow. The argument has some force, but is not very persuasive. The program has been in existence for almost 40 years, but most of the provinces that were net contributors at the beginning are still net contributors today, and the beneficiaries are the same as well. For Alberta, British Columbia, and Ontario, the program of equalization payments is an insurance policy that would never have been chosen out of self-interest, and would not be chosen now. The insurance argument is particularly fragile and unconvincing with regard to Quebec, which may no longer be part of Canada at some future time when Quebec is prosperous enough to be a net contributor to the program.

The administrative cost of the Canadian program of equalization payments

The equalization program consists, essentially, in the issuing of seven cheques a year by the Federal-Provincial Relations and Social Policy Department of the Ministry of Finance at an administrative cost of less than five million dollars.[16] The full overhead cost of the program includes the expenditure of time by politicians and civil servants in negotiating how large the cheques will be: the effort of each recipient province to tilt the equalization formula to its advantage, of each non-recipient province to minimize the cost of the program, and of the federal government to resolve disputes. Regardless, the full cost of administration is probably low by comparison with the cost of many other federal programs.

To summarize, one is in no better position to assess the net effect of the equalization program on the efficiency in the economy as a whole than to assess its effect upon the overall distribution of income. There are forces pushing the economy every which way, their magnitudes are difficult if not impossible to ascertain and the net impacts remain unknown. There may be some gain in efficiency from the improvement in the allocation among provinces of the mobile factors of production, but that may be illusory in an environment where other policies tend to restrict migration from the have-not provinces to the rest of the country. There may be a gain in efficiency from the reduction in the total excess burden of taxation in Canada as provincial tax rates are equalized, but that, too, may be illusory, because provinces are encouraged by the program to distort their tax structures to maximize entitlement for transfers from the federal government. Other than in Quebec, the cultivation of local specificity seems to be a red herring. If provincial administration reflects local tastes and interests—a less than obvious proposition—then it does so regardless of whether equalization payments are provided.

If there is a case for equalization payments on grounds of efficiency, that case is probably stronger for the very poor provinces than for provinces with incomes per head that are not too far off the national average. In particular, without equalization payments, the attempt by poor provinces to provide national standards of expenditure on health care might entail an especially large excess burden of taxation. For provinces with incomes close to the national average, the benefit from the transfer under the equalization program might be outweighed by the cost of the distortion in provincial tax rates to maximize the size of the transfer. In general, on grounds of efficiency, as on grounds of equality, the case for equalization is speculative and inconclusive. The balance of the argument may go either way.

Part IV: Equity

O N GROUNDS OF EQUALITY AND EFFICIENCY, the case for the Canadian program of equalization payments is weak. If the program were to be abolished lock, stock, and barrel (perhaps over a few years to provide time for the governments of the recipient provinces to adjust to the change), there need be no significant increase or decrease in the Canadian national income, and no significant widening or narrowing of the distribution of income (broadly defined to include provision of public services) among Canadians. Abolish equalization payments and the Canadian national income may go up, down, or remain the same. Abolish equalization payments and the distribution of income among all Canadians may widen, narrow, or remain the same. Thus, the burden of justification would seem to fall on equity. The question becomes whether a program of equalization payments might be warranted on some principle of fairness, order, or good government. The question becomes whether Canadian society was less just, decent, honourable, and orderly before the program of equalization payments was introduced, and whether it would become so again if the program were abolished or substantially changed.

The logic of equity

Equity is the peaceful virtue. It is an essential ingredient of a community where people live according to rules specifying the occupants of the ranks in the hierarchies of business and government and allocating the national income among people. It is the peaceful virtue because the alternative to allocation by rules is the costly and dangerous squabble to determine who takes what, leading in the end to war of all against all over the allocation of goods and services. In the words of James Buchanan in the classic article on fiscal equity from which the example in table II.3 was taken, the essential role of equity in public expenditure and taxation[17]

> has been so widely recognized that it has not been expressly stated at all times, but rather implicitly assumed. Whether or not this principle is consistent with maximizing social utility, it is essential as a guide to the operation of a liberal democratic state, stemming from the same basic principle of equality of individuals before the law.

As a criterion for taxation, equity becomes the principle of "horizontal equity" that "equals should be taxed equally," that people should be taxed the same if their incomes are the same, regardless of how their incomes are acquired. One person may acquire his income as a lawyer, another as a brick layer, another from ownership of bonds, another from ownership of property. All should pay the equal amounts of tax if they earn equal amounts of income.[18] In the end, horizontal equity is connected to property rights as two sides of the same coin. People can only be said to possess property if that property is secure from expropriation by the government, directly or through discriminatory taxation. Taxation constrained by the principle of horizontal equity preserves property rights. Unconstrained by the principle of horizontal equity, the power to tax is indeed the power to destroy. The purpose of horizontal equity is to defend citizens against victimization by governments and to defend society against the internecine rivalry that the possibility of victimization would entail, lest forces be released that lead in the end to the disintegration of democratic government. Without broad, impersonal principles of taxation, every person becomes the enemy of every other person in a general scramble to evade the burden of taxation, the tax gathering agency is beset by irresistible pressures to favour one person over another, and politics is corrupted by the temptation to buy votes of particular people or groups of people with promises of low taxation. To be sure, these vices are never avoided altogether, but they would run out of control if the principle of horizontal equity were ignored and *ad hominem* taxation were to become the norm. Horizontal equity is the one clear principle in a context where the alternative is chaos.

If people earning equal incomes are not taxed equally, then what, one might ask, should their taxes be? Should one person pay less tax than another because his brother-in-law is a Member of Parliament, or should he pay more tax because the other threatens to raise a rumpus or leave the country unless his tax bill is reduced? The principle that equals should be taxed equally may be fuzzy at the edges (as in allowance for marital status) and it may be violated on occasion (as in ad hoc government aid to industry), but it is universally recognized because there is no alternative.

Equity is distinct from popularity. A program may be widely, even unanimously supported, but inequitable all the same. There may be considerable support in the general population for a program of public subsidization of investment by progressive firms, but the program may still be inequitable because it cannot be administered without generating political pressures by would-be recipients, and without turning people against their neighbours in a general scramble for public largesse. The essence of equity is that, once an equitable rule is adopted, there can be no further dispute within the domain of application of the rule about who is entitled to what, or, since disputes can never be banished altogether, fewer and less acrimonious disputes than under any alternative rule. Property is equitable in this sense of the term; "horizontal equity" is even more so.

Equity may also be distinguished from justice. Equity is a characteristic of rules; justice pertains to the manner in which rules are applied. Equity is a virtue of laws; justice is a virtue of judges. So defined, equity is one among several criteria for evaluating public policy, and is never in itself decisive. Alternative rules may be equally equitable. A relatively inequitable rule may on occasion be preferred to a relatively equitable rule because the former is more conducive to efficiency or equality.

Equalization as equity

The Canadian program of equalization payments is sometimes defended as the natural extension of horizontal equity to federal-provincial relations. If it is proper for equals to be taxed equally in federal and provincial taxation, then, so the argument goes, it should also be proper for otherwise identical people in different provinces to pay the same rates of tax for the same quality of public services, except in the event that a province chooses to impose higher (or lower) taxes to provide more expensive (or less expensive) public services. Equalization is to provinces as horizontal equity is to people. Justification for the one is justification for the other.

But is that really so? Can one be sure that the benefits of horizontal equity in taxation extend automatically to equalization payments? To get to the bottom of this question, it is necessary to examine the analogy between horizontal equity and equalization to see how far the logic of the one applies to the other. In this enterprise, we must take special care about the connotations of words. Equalization sounds right. Equity sounds right. Drenched as they are with philosophic significance and profound academic approbation, equity and equalization become self-evidently desirable. We must do better than that. We must test the concept of equalization against public purpose to be sure that our warm feelings about the term are not misleading and illusory. We must try to specify what happens in the absence of a program of equalization payments and to decide whether the result is really undesirable.

Are the dire consequences of the abandonment of horizontal equity in the taxation of people really to be expected from the abandonment of equalization payments by the federal government to the provinces? Or is the association of equalization payments with horizontal equity like a "persuasive definition" that suggests a proposition without actually establishing that it is true? There are, in fact, some substantial differences: First, as the principle of horizontal equity has no application across countries, there is some question as to whether it should apply across provinces either. Second, unlike horizontal equity in its domain, equalization is not the only available principle for federal-provincial relations. Third, Section 36(2) contains no unique and well-specified rule for transfers. It can be "frivolous" in its effects on provinces and people.

The Canadian program of equalization payments may intensify the scramble over privilege that the rules of equity are intended to moderate. Each of these points will be discussed in turn.

A major difference between horizontal equity and equal rates of taxation among provinces is that the former pertains to the treatment of two people by one government, while the latter pertains to the treatment of two people by two separate governments. For the preservation of a democratic society, it matters a great deal if the government of the United Kingdom taxes otherwise identical citizens at different rates, but it does not really matter if citizens of the United Kingdom are taxed at different rates than identically-placed citizens of India. One might say that one country or the other is acting inexpediently, but one would not be inclined to say that the principle of horizontal equity is violated, for the alleged consequences of a violation of horizontal equity would not be forthcoming in that case. The question at hand is whether, in a country where the powers of the provinces are sanctioned by a constitution, differences in provincial tax rates on similar people in different provinces are like differences in tax rates between the United Kingdom and India or like differences in tax rates on similarly-situated people within the United Kingdom.

To ask this question is to answer it. Obviously jurisdiction matters. Just as there is nobody for me to plead with, bribe, or vote against for compensation from another country if that country's tax rates are lower than the tax rates in my country, so too there is nobody for me to plead with, bribe, or vote against for compensation from another province if that province's tax rates are lower than the tax rates in my province. To be sure, the federal government can make interprovincial transfers, but the dangers in the exercise of that power are no less real in the presence of equalization payments. The threat to democracy would seem to be genuine when one government treats equals unequally. Different treatment by different governments may have adverse consequences on efficiency and equality, but not on horizontal equity as the term is commonly understood. The rivalry among citizens seeking to shift the burden of taxation onto their fellow citizens and the potential for victimization of citizens by the government when identically-placed citizens within the same jurisdiction are taxed at different rates is unlikely to arise if residents of Manitoba are taxed at different rates by the government of Manitoba than residents of Alberta are taxed by the government of Alberta.

Look back at the example in case (ii) of table II.3. Without equalization payments, the provincial tax rates are 14.3 percent in province A and 25 percent in province B, and there is no federal taxation. When equalization payments are introduced, the tax rate in province B is reduced to 18.2 percent, and there is introduced a federal income tax at a rate of 2.5 percent, so that total, federal and provincial, tax rates become 16.8 percent in province A and 20.7 percent in province B. Should this narrowing of tax rates be seen as a move toward horizontal equity? It surely is if the definition of horizontal equity is extended to cover tax rates in different provinces, but the question then becomes whether equity so defined is desirable for the reason stated by Buchanan in the quotation above, or for any other reason apart from equality and efficiency. The question becomes whether a narrowing of the gap between tax rates on like people in different provinces has effects comparable to the establishment of genuine horizontal equity—to a lessening of discrimination in taxation among similarly-situated people within one jurisdiction—and whether there is any reasonable sense of the word discrimination in which province A or the federal government can be said to discriminate against residents of province B in the event that province B imposes a higher tax rate upon its residents in a regime without equalization payments.

Equality among the tax rates of the provinces (for a given quality of public services) differs from horizontal equity in that it is not the only, or even the most obvious, principle of federal-provincial finance. There is a simpler and very much more precise competitor, the principle that each province pays with its own tax revenue for the services it provides, that "each tub floats on its own bottom." The "each tub" principle can be interpreted so strictly as to preclude all transfers from the federal government to the provinces, but it might be stretched to allow for joint cost programs, such as the federal matching grant for expenditure on welfare, or for transfers per person as in Established Programs Financing. But the important consideration here is not the relative merits of the "each tub" principle and the principle of equalizing tax rates across provinces. The important consideration is that the principle of equalizing tax rates across the provinces is not a unique and indispensable bulwark against chaos, comparable to horizontal equity in ordinary income taxation. It is a principle that may but need not be chosen. Public order did not break down, and interprovincial rivalry was not more intense than it is today, in the bad old days before the Canadian program of equalization payments was established, and there is no reason to believe that public order would break down if equalization payments were abolished today. Other federal countries, such as the United States, survive without equalization payments. That equalization payments are not necessarily efficient or equalizing adds weight to the argument that they are not an essential ingredient of individual rights or public order, comparable to the principle of horizontal equity in ordinary taxation.

On the contrary, a program of equalization payments may well provoke precisely the dissension, ill-will, rent seeking and blackmail among provinces, and ultimately among citizens in the different provinces, that the principle of horizontal equity is intended to avoid. The reason is that the amounts of equalization payments to the different provinces are always up for grabs, always the subject of negotiation between the federal government and the provinces. There is negotiation over the number of tax bases to be equalized. Only three taxes—the personal income tax, the corporate income tax, and the succession duty—were recognized in 1957 when the equalization program was introduced. Then the number of tax bases was gradually increased, until today there are 33 bases in the formula with a host of special provisions for a variety of reasons. There is negotiation over the representative province in the formula. At first it was the average of what were the two wealthiest provinces: Ontario and British Columbia. Then it expanded to all provinces. Then it contracted to five provinces: Quebec, Ontario, Manitoba, Saskatchewan and British Columbia. There is negotiation over provincial income from energy resources, especially over the extent to which a province can withdraw potential tax revenue from consideration in the formula by converting it into low prices for energy users in the province. There is negotiation over the measurement of tax revenue and tax base because, for many items, no uniquely-correct and altogether-undisputable right procedure can be identified. Millions of dollars of transfers to this or that province may depend on the choice among equally-plausible interpretations. Entitlements become the subject of lengthy and acrimonious bargaining among provinces and between the provinces and the federal government. It is impossible to tell at a distance to what extent the formula drives the outcome and to what extent the outcome drives the formula.

There is room for dispute over the translation of Section 36(2) into a precise equalization formula. Section 36(2) does not require, as an examination of the formula would suggest, that provinces be able to acquire equal revenues at equal rates of tax. It requires that provinces "have sufficient revenues to provide reasonably comparable levels of public services at reasonably comparable levels of taxation." Nothing in Section 36(2) identifies "sufficient revenues" with equal revenue per head in the different provinces, or suggests that a province where services are especially costly should be provided with no more than the average revenue per head in the country as a whole. As already mentioned in Part I, a reasonable interpretation of section 36(2) might take account of price level differences among the provinces, of the extra cost of providing a given quality of medical care in a sparsely settled province, of the extra cost of welfare in a province with large numbers of poor and unemployed people, and of the extra cost of medical care in a province where a great many people retire. Nor can the partial equalization in the Canadian formula be justified with reference to the constitutional mandate. Section 36(2) mandates equality, not partial equality. Equality might be obtained a) by providing large enough subsidies to all but the most prosperous provinces that every province's revenue per head would be the same at the average provincial tax rates on all tax bases, a procedure requiring a substantial increase in the amount of equalization payments and in the rate of federal taxation to finance them, or b) by replacing federal transfers with compulsory transfers from rich provinces to poor provinces on the understanding that rich provinces would be designated by their tax bases rather than by income per head (that is, by replacing the present "equalization up" rule of equation I.3 with the "net" rule of equation I.2), or c) by raising all provincial revenue with a poll tax, so that rates are equal among provinces by definition.

Emphasis on the discrepancy between the constitutional mandate and the Canadian equalization formula is not intended to suggest that the formula should be modified to conform to the constitutional mandate. On the contrary, there is reason to believe that a program designed to reflect Section 36(2) accurately would be less equitable on balance than the program as it is today, for the opportunities for conflict among the provinces over the interpretation of the constitutional mandate would be enormous. The discrepancy is emphasized to demonstrate that the potentiality for discord and discrimination is already considerable. Provinces can always find discrepancies between the constitutional mandate and the actual program, according to which they receive too little under the program, or pay too much.

It is at least arguable that what appears at first as redistribution among the provinces in accordance with reasonably well-specified rules may in reality be a great unprincipled squabble over federal largesse. One does not have to be especially cynical to suspect that the consequences for the different provinces and social classes were not altogether ignored when the Canadian program of equalization payments was designed, and that struggles among potential winners and losers as the formula is changed from time to time have some of the features and some of the consequences of departures from horizontal equity in ordinary taxation.

My impression is that the history of the formula is the outcome of a complex mixture of reason and expediency. It would not be altogether wrong to say that the formula was gradually adjusted to reflect the principles of equalization as expressed in Section 36(2) of the constitution. Nor, I suspect, would it be altogether wrong to say that those who adjusted the formula were fully aware of the distributive implications of the changes as they occurred and that the federal government was pressured, even bullied, to adopt the formula we have today.

Ultimately, horizontal equity is about the rule of law—the maintenance of "a government of rules, not of men." A program of equalization payments would be equitable on balance if there were likely to be less competition among the provinces over federal largesse with a program in place than if every province had to take full responsibility for its own public expenditure. A program of equalization payments would be equitable if it were so exact in its implications about who is entitled to what, and so indisputably fair in its effect upon people in different provinces, that there would be less interprovincial rivalry than if every tub had to float on its own bottom. There is reason to fear the opposite. The gap between the wording of Section 36(2) of the Canadian constitution and the Canadian formula, the room for manipulation of the formula to affect the entitlements of the recipient provinces, and the prospect that the formula may be changed again to favour this or that province, may all give rise to precisely that competition among the provinces that an equitable program would be designed to forestall. All these considerations speak *against* equalization payments as a means to equity, not *for* them as is often supposed.

The completion of horizontal equity in federal taxation

Even if one rejects the argument for equalization payments from the straightforward analogy between horizontal equity in taxation within a single jurisdiction and uniformity of tax rates among jurisdictions, one might still argue for some form of federal-provincial transfer as compensation for a departure from horizontal equity when provincial revenues are protected from ordinary federal taxation by the rule that "the crown cannot tax the crown" as set out in different words in Section 125 of the Canadian constitution.

Horizontal equity warrants "broad base" taxation covering all sources of income. It is horizontally inequitable if all of one person's income is subject to tax, while part of another person's income is exempt. All of one's income should be subject to federal taxation, including that which accrues directly (as wages or dividends) and that which accrues indirectly through the intermediary of the provincial government. In particular, a person's share of the revenue from provincially-owned natural resources should, ideally, be looked upon as part of his income because, without that revenue, higher tax rates would be required to finance public services in the province. A person's share of that revenue should be counted as part of his income in the assessment of federal income tax. Barring that (for it would be inconvenient for the federal government to tax people on revenue accruing to the government of the province where they live), provincial governments might be taxed directly. Baring that (for Section 125 of the Canadian Constitution forbids federal taxation of the provinces), provinces with little revenue from their own sources might be subsidized. The argument is convoluted but not altogether wrong, though it is questionable whether the argument points to institutions remotely resembling the Canadian program of equalization payments.

A barrel of petroleum is pumped from a well in Alberta. The well head price of petroleum is $20 a barrel (over and above the cost of extraction), and the rate of federal income taxation is 30 percent. If the well is owned privately by a resident of Alberta, the $20 is counted as part of his before-tax income and he is taxed $6 by the federal government, leaving him with an extra $14 to spend. Alternatively, if the well is owned by the province of Alberta, the appearance of the extra barrel of petroleum enables the province to reduce ordinary provincial tax revenue by the full $20, leaving the residents of the province with an extra $20 to spend, money on which no federal tax would be collected. Thus, building on an analogy with horizontal equity, it would seem reasonable for the federal government to impose an extra $6 of taxation upon the residents of Alberta, or upon the government of Alberta which would then have to raise an extra $6 from the residents of the province to maintain the existing level of public services. As that is blocked by Section 125, there may be a case for compensating all other provinces for the implicit tax exemption to Alberta.

Before considering who might be compensated and how large the compensation ought to be, it should be noted that the problem is wider than the taxation of provincially-owned natural resources. The argument for federal taxation of provincial revenue, or for an equivalent subsidization of certain provinces, extends to all "source based" as distinct from "person based" taxation. The essence of the distinction in the present context is that provincial source-based taxation lowers pre-tax incomes of the owners of the tax base and thereby lowers the amount of federal tax that must be paid. Thus, for example, even if petroleum is privately owned, a provincial tax on the production of petroleum lowers the incomes of its owners within the province and thereby lowers their federal tax bill. In fact, provincial taxation of the output of petroleum at a rate of 25 percent is financially equivalent to provincial ownership of 25 percent of the output of petroleum. A provincial sales tax can be thought of as source-based for some purposes, though the ultimate incidence is hard to trace.[19]

The problem now becomes to determine what transfers, if any, from the federal government to certain provinces might be warranted on the working assumption that the federal government should, but cannot, tax each person's source-based income accruing to the province where one lives. The way to deal with this problem is to trace the consequences of federal taxation and to see how they might be replicated by some other means. If the federal government could tax the provinces according to their source-based revenue, it would, of course, be taxing all provinces to some extent, because no province is without any source-based revenue at all. If all provinces, rich or poor, had the same proportion of source-based revenue, then all provinces would lose the same proportion of their revenue, specifically, the product of their share of source-based revenue and the average rate of federal income tax. At the same time, the federal government would be acquiring additional revenue and would be able to adjust expenditure or taxation (where the deficit is counted as a form of taxation) accordingly. If the federal government chose to reduce taxes, then people in the different provinces would benefit in proportion to the federal taxes they would otherwise pay. Indeed, if the proportion of source-based revenue to total taxable income were the same for all provinces, the entire operation would be awash. Provinces would be taxed on their source-based revenue, but taxpayers would gain as much from the reduction in federal taxation as they would lose from the increase in provincial taxation to cover the province's tax bill to the federal government. And as nobody would be made better off or worse off by the transaction, no federal transfers to the provinces would be warranted.

This clean result rests on assumptions which are unlikely to hold in practice. It is highly unlikely that the gain to residents in each and every province from the untaxability by the federal government of provincial resource revenue and other source-based revenue is just matched by the extra federal taxation required to make up for the lost revenue. There is also some question about how the missing federal revenue might have been used. It might have been devoted to the equivalent of equal per capita grants to all provinces, in which case some federal grant to the have not provinces might be warranted as compensation. Among provinces, there are winners and losers, though it is by no means evident who the winners might be.

What is evident is that these considerations do not warrant anything like the present Canadian equalization program. First, as provincial revenue would be linked to private income, the full equalization as mandated by Section 36(2) would be altogether unwarranted. At most, a proportion of the difference between provinces in revenue per head might be made up by federal transfers. Second, the perfection of horizontal equity would warrant federal transfers from resource-rich provinces to resource-poor provinces, regardless of whether, all things considered, the residents of the provinces are rich or poor. It might warrant a federal subsidy to Ontario and Manitoba, but not to Alberta or Newfoundland.

The Alberta-Ontario problem

Another aspect of equity is that a program should not be frivolous in its impact on the distribution of income. A rule that enriches one person or impoverishes another for no good reason is bound to be changed from time to time as its implications are recognized, and the prospect of change is likely to involve precisely that competition, rent seeking and jockeying for advantage one would hope to avoid through the establishment of equitable rules. The Canadian program of equalization payments is frivolous in its impact on the welfare of the donor provinces because it allows fortuitous events to cause redistributions among them—unintended redistributions which in no way conform to purposes of the program. An event that increases the revenue of any donor province triggers an increase in the transfer from the remaining donor provinces to the recipient provinces. This is so even if the event is harmful to the residents of the remaining donor provinces, provided only that the harm causes no significant reduction in provincial revenue. In particular, when the representative province in the equalization formula was an average of all provinces, an increase in the world price of petroleum would set off a transfer of income from Ontario to the Maritimes and Quebec, despite the fact that the increase in the world price of petroleum was just as harmful to the people of Ontario as to the people of the Maritimes and Quebec. This consideration was important in the switch from the all-province standard to the to the five-province standard, excluding Alberta. To get at the essence of the Alberta-Ontario problem, it is convenient to imagine a stylized Canada with three provinces, Alberta and Ontario, which are the "have" provinces, and one "have not" province that receives equalization payments. The population of this Canada is 25 million, 2.5 million in Alberta, 10 million in Ontario and 12.5 million in the "have not" province. Provincial revenue from petroleum is one of the categories in the equalization formula, and Alberta is the only province with revenue in this category. Provincial ownership of petroleum revenue is equivalent to a provincial tax of 100 percent, and, as only Alberta has petroleum revenue, that is the national average rate too. Now suppose that an increase in the world price of petroleum leads to an increase of $1 billion, equivalent to $400 per person, in the revenue of the province of Alberta. Since Alberta contains 10 percent of the Canadian population and is the only province with petroleum revenue, the average provincial revenue must increase by $40 per person, and total equalization payments to the recipient province must increase by $500 million (40 x 12.5 million). None of this would be harmful to the residents of Ontario if Canada had opted for the net formula in equation I.2 because the increased entitlement of the recipient province would then be financed from the extra revenue in Alberta. With the "equalization up" formula of equation I.3 that we actually employ, the federal government pays recipient provinces out of ordinary federal tax revenue, of which, let us suppose, three-fifths is raised, mostly by personal and corporate taxation, in Ontario. The federal tax bill to the people of Ontario must increase by $300 million, even though the residents of Ontario must also pay more for the petroleum they buy. Though the whole process began by a windfall gain to Alberta, the residents of Alberta pay a relatively small share of the extra equalization payment because the taxation of petroleum yields a relatively small share of federal revenue. While it is unlikely that there remain anomalies as egregious as this in the Canadian equalization program, the possibility of fortuitous redistribution among the donor provinces has not been eliminated altogether by the change from the all-province standard to the five-province standard in the determination of entitlements to equalization payments.

The tax-back problem

This is really an aspect of the Alberta-Ontario problem. If any recipient province has the lion's share of a particular tax base, it becomes virtually impossible for that province to increase its revenue by raising its tax rate on that base, for the increase in the province's tax revenue automatically reduces its entitlement to equalization payments, almost dollar for dollar. The province would have every incentive to reduce, or even eliminate, its tax on that base, for equalization payments would make up the lost revenue. To counteract this perverse incentive, the federal government has adopted a 70 percent rule. If a recipient province accounts for 70 percent or more of the total production of a natural resource, revenues arising from that resource and subject to equalization are reduced by 30 percent in all provinces, reducing the loss in the entitlement of the province with the large resource concentration from what it would otherwise be. The beneficiaries of this rule are Quebec, through its application to asbestos, and Saskatchewan, through its application to potash. The rule is, of course, very arbitrary in the sense that it is one of a large number of rules that might have been established with different distributional consequences. For example, by analogy with the federal response to provincial variations in provision of health care, provinces with large amounts of natural resources could be assumed to impose a certain minimal tax on these resources, regardless of whether they actually impose that tax or not. An additional arbitrariness is introduced by the imposition of ceilings and floors to the amounts of equalization payments that any province may receive and the amount that the federal government must pay. You cannot go directly from the general principle of equalization to the specification of each province's entitlement. Subsidiary rules had to be negotiated in circumstances where it would be evident to all who the gainers and the losers of each possible rule would be.

The treatment of natural resources

There is a split personality within the Canadian Constitution over the ownership of natural resources. The Constitution decrees in its wisdom that a) by Section 92A(4), resources belong to the provinces which have the sole right to tax them, and b) by Section 36(2), the federal government may seize the resource revenue indirectly by subsidizing provinces without resource revenue. If Section 36(2) means what it says, then provincial tax rates should be the same in all provinces for a given level of services regardless of whether a province has natural resource revenue. Deficit provinces must therefore be compensated by the federal government. The equalization formula specifies the amount of compensation due. The federal government may not tax away the resource revenue of the provincial governments but must replicate the effect of taxation on the welfare of the residents of the resource-rich provinces. The federal government must do in an inefficient and round about way what it may not do efficiently and directly.

In general, there would seem to be three main views about how natural resource revenues might be treated in a program of equalization payments: i) taking the Canadian Constitution at its word, one might say that natural resources belong entirely to the provinces and that the federal government has no business reappropriating any provincial revenue from natural resources, not by taxation of resource-rich provinces, nor by complicated manoeuvres, such as equalization payments, that compensate the have-not provinces to some extent, ii) Sections 92A(4) and 125 may be seen as a great mistake that has to be corrected by compensating transfers from the federal government to resource-deficit provinces, so that revenue per capita from natural resources is the same in all provinces regardless of the initial allocation of the resources themselves. The fruit must be shared equally no matter which province happens to own the tree, and iii) resources may be seen as owned by the provinces with this exception: that the public's share of natural resource revenue should be treated as private income in the assessment of liability for the personal and corporate income taxation by the federal government, or, equivalently, that the federal government should tax the resource-rich provinces (or deny them subsidies granted to other provinces) to compensate for the lost revenue from the federal income tax. On this view, the resource-rich provinces would have to make up the lost revenue by imposing extra taxation on their residents who would, in the end, be no better off than if taxed directly on their share of provincial resource revenue. As argued above, this last view might warrant some equalization payments, but less than at present and based on a very different formula than is used now or could be justified by Section 36(2).

The spending power and its implications

The split personality within the Canadian constitution is not limited to the ownership of natural resources. The federal government is blocked by the Canadian constitution from expenditure and taxation in areas of provincial jurisdiction, but it is unblocked again by a principle in Canadian constitutional law called the doctrine of the "spending power." The core of the doctrine is an analogy between a person and a government. Just as a person may give gifts to whomever he pleases, so too may a government. That a government cannot give to one person or province without at the same time taking from other people or provinces through the intermediary of the tax system is deemed to be irrelevant. When you give me a gift, it is financed out of income that you have earned. When a government gives me a gift, it is also financed out of income that you have earned. The spending power allows the federal government to ignore these considerations.

An early and influential statement of the doctrine of the spending power is by F.R. Scott:

> All public monies ... belong to the Crown. The Crown is a person capable of making gifts or contracts like any other person, to whomsoever it chooses to benefit. The recipient may be another government or private individuals. The only constitutional requirement for Crown gifts is that they that they must have the approval of Parliament or legislature. This being obtained, the Prince may distribute his largesse at will. ... Moreover the Crown may attach conditions to the gift, failure to observe which will cause its discontinuance. These simple but significant powers exist in our constitutional law though no mention of them can be found in the BNA Acts. They derive from the doctrines of the Royal Prerogative and the common law.[20]

The validity of the doctrine has subsequently been recognized by the Canadian Supreme Court. "The Court should not, under the 'overriding principle of federalism' supervise the federal government's exercise of the spending power in order to protect the autonomy of the provinces." (Reference re: Canada Assistance Plan (BC), [1991] 2SCR, p. 530). The spending power does not confer on the federal government the right to spend directly within the jurisdiction of the provincial governments. Instead, it confers on the federal government the authority to bribe the province with its own money, saying in effect to each province that, unless you do exactly as I say with the gift I am giving you, I shall withdraw the gift, but tax you all the same for your share of the cost of gifts to others less uncooperative than yourself.

The emergence of this peculiar doctrine in Canadian constitutional law is a consequence, in my opinion, of the growing discrepancy between the federal-provincial division of powers in the BNA Act of 1867 and the division of powers that seems to be appropriate today. It is, of course, highly unlikely for a given division of powers to remain appropriate over a period of 125 years. Any division of powers becomes increasingly cumbersome and inappropriate as time goes by. The doctrine of the spending power is the means by which the discrepancy was circumvented. Especially since the Second World War, the federal government—probably in accordance with the preferences of the majority of Canadians—sought to establish national standards for health care, higher education, and other public services, but was thwarted by a constitution that decreed health, education, and welfare to be under the jurisdiction of the provincial governments. The provincial governments, on the other hand, were in a poor position to finance the functions of government they had been assigned, except at prohibitively high excess burdens of taxation, but, like all governments everywhere, were loath to divest themselves of their powers.

With all paths blocked, the constitutional lawyers invented a highway. The spending power permitted the federal government to establish national standards through an elaborate network of transfers to the provinces including a fixed transfer per head called Established Program Financing, a 50 percent subsidy of expenditure on welfare for the poor under the Canada Assistance Plan, the program of equalization payments and a wide range of *ad hoc* transfers. The federal government places conditions on its transfers, national standards as they are called, creating a uniformity of services among the provinces that destroys all rationale for provincial jurisdiction except as a means of aggrandizement for the provincial governments themselves, and except in Quebec where language is important.

But the highway was too broad, accommodating not only the authority to establish national standards but the authority to transfer income to provinces or people for any purpose whatever, regardless of the allocation of powers under the constitution. The spending power pits every province against every other province in a great rent seeking jamboree, a contest in which the province of Quebec is especially fortunate because the threat of separation is a better bargaining chip than any other province can command. The exercise of the spending power by the federal government becomes inherently inequitable because it substitutes negotiation for principle. Instead of specifying the powers of the provincial governments and allowing them to act unimpeded and unbribed within their jurisdictions, we have evolved a system of government by federal-provincial negotiation—an intensification of the pork barrel politics in the United States—in which the goodies go to the parties who can make the most extreme and most credible threats, a system which is, in my opinion, in no small measure responsible for the constitutional crisis that is upon us now.

Two opposing pictures can be drawn of the Canadian equalization program. Equalization payments may be seen as a natural extension of the principle of horizontal equity that "equals should be taxed equally," the ultimate rationale for this principle being to preserve order in society by allocating tax burdens so fairly that everyone is prepared to accept the burden imposed upon them without recourse to political activity to shift their burden onto others, and, especially, without recourse to violence to impose what they see as a more appropriate allocation among people of the cost of public services. Equalization payments may also be seen as ingredient in an elaborate system of bribes from the federal government to the governments of the provinces, a great pork barrel scheme worked out between the federal government and the provinces, but justified to the Canadian people by noble ideals and supported by politicians who, to preserve their mental health, must acquire the knack of believing fervently in the justice of what they find expedient to do. It is difficult if not impossible to say with assurance where on the continuum from high principle to low cunning the program of equalization payments ought rightly to be placed.[21]

As with equality and efficiency, one cannot say definitively whether the virtue of equity is or is not promoted by the Canadian program of equalization payments. My hunch is that it is not.

Part V: Reform

THE REFORM OF EQUALIZATION PAYMENTS cannot be examined in a vacuum. The Canadian program is a complex institution with linkages to other policies and programs. Its rationale is, to a considerable extent, to neutralize the adverse consequences of other programs and of various unfortunate provisions of the Canadian constitution, especially the placement of natural resources under provincial rather than federal jurisdiction. Assessment of the Canadian program, and of the benefits and costs of possible reforms, must depend as well on whether Quebec remains part of Canada. It is said, over and over again, that Canada is a compromise between French and English, but it is not always appreciated how the compromise is manifest in the institutions of Canada today, or what is implied about the organization of English Canada in the event that Quebec chooses to go. In particular, it is not always appreciated that the appropriate division of powers between the federal and provincial governments might be very different for a Canada without Quebec. If the program of equalization payments is what it is because of the present division of powers between the federal and provincial governments, and if the separation of Quebec warrants a new division of powers, then the case for equalization payments and the assessment of proposals for reform might be very different, too.[22]

At the root of many of the problems discussed in this paper is the principle that the return to common property should accrue to everybody, regardless of where within the country they choose to reside, for resources are wasted if I am denied my share of the return unless I go somewhere or do something that does not in itself constitute the most productive use of the resources at my disposal. Labour and other mobile factors of production are misallocated when people migrate to Alberta to acquire a share of oil revenue, or when people migrate to other rich provinces to take advantage of low provincial tax rates. There are two main correctives for the inefficiency in provincial ownership of common property. Common property can be nationalized, or provinces without common property can be compensated by the central government. Natural resources and the redistribution of income among Canadians, including the provision of welfare and medical care, can be placed under the jurisdiction of the federal government, or, alternatively, the federal government can compensate provinces without their share of natural resources or rich people. Of course, not all departures from efficiency ought to be corrected; the cure may, in practice, be worse than the disease. The choice between federalization and compensation depends very much on the force of the local specificity argument, and that in turn is considerably stronger in a country with Quebec than in a country without Quebec. Where a strong provincial government is thought necessary for the preservation of the French language in Quebec, there is a case for provincial jurisdiction over a considerable range of activities notwithstanding the inefficiency involved, but there is also a case for federal programs to mitigate the inefficiency that provincial jurisdiction entails. This is no longer a consideration in a Canada without Quebec. The local specificity argument becomes very much weaker, the case for federal jurisdiction becomes stronger, and there is less reason to tolerate the fiscal contortions that compensation through equalization payments entail.

With these general considerations in mind, five possible changes to the equalization program will be examined: the replacement of the present equalization formula with a macro formula, province-to-province equalization, partial equalization, deconstitutionalization, and abolition.

Macro formulas

As discussed in Part I, a macro formula assigns equalization payments according to a province's shortfall in gross domestic product rather than according to its shortfall in average tax base. The entitlement, E_i, of province i becomes

$$E_i = \textit{the larger of } \{0, t_c(y_c - y_i)P_i\} \tag{V.1}$$

where y_i is the gross domestic product per head in province i, y_c is gross domestic product per head in the country as a whole, P_i is the population of province i, and t_c is the average provincial tax rate, measured as the ratio over all provinces together of total provincial revenue to total gross domestic product. As with the present formula, this version of the macro formula provides an equalization payment that is positive or zero, but never negative; a subsidy or nothing, but no tax. Once again, transfers to the designated provinces would be financed out of ordinary federal tax revenue.

The macro formula has two principal advantages over the present formula. First, and most important in my opinion, a macro formula is more likely to funnel money to provinces that are actually poor. As a rule, a province where people are poor can be expected to have a low tax base per head, but the correlation is imperfect and a poor province could in some circumstances have a high tax base. This could occur in a province where most people are uneducated and unproductive or where there is little land or capital per head but where there is larger than average supply of natural resources. Such a province could be classified as a "have" province under the usual equalization formula if average provincial tax rates are higher on natural resources than on other sources of income. A macro formula is less frivolous than the present formula and less dependent on irrelevant aspects of provincial tax codes. Second, a macro formula presents the provinces with far less opportunity to influence their entitlements to equalization payments by modifying their tax codes in inefficient ways. A recipient province could still affect its entitlement slightly because the average provincial tax rate increases whenever any province's tax rate increases, but there is probably not much mileage in that. With the present formula, a province can increase its entitlement without changing total revenue by raising the rate on a deficit base and lowering the rate on a surplus base. With a macro formula, that option would be closed. Nor would there be much scope for hiding a part of the base of the equalization formula. With the present formula, a province can increase its entitlement by, for instance, lowering the price of domestically-produced electricity within the province. With a macro formula, a province would need to reduce its entire measured gross domestic product.

Against the macro formula, it may be argued that the connection between equalization and horizontal equity would be severed to some extent and that there would be no allowance for the social cost of tax collection. If the social cost of taxation is low for some forms of taxation and high for others, then the present formula may do better than a macro formula in subsidizing provinces that are poorly endowed in low-cost sources of taxation. Though formally valid, the argument is not, in my opinion, very convincing. It seems a safer bet to focus upon provinces that are known to be relatively poor—to take the word "equalization" seriously—than to go for a formula that might possibly favour provinces where the social cost of tax collection is high.

Province-to-province transfers

Regardless of how deficit provinces are identified, equalization payments could be financed by taxing the rich provinces directly rather than from the general revenue of the federal government, by "net" equalization rather than by "equalizing up." The federal transfer to the governments of Prince Edward Island and Quebec would be financed by federal taxation of the governments of Alberta and Ontario. Province-to-province equalization could be conducted with reference to the present equalization formula or with reference to a macro formula. With a macro formula, each province's entitlement under province-to-province equalization becomes

$$E_i = t_c(y_c - y_i)P_i \tag{V.2}$$

where the meanings of the symbols are the same as in the ordinary macro formula in equation V.1 above. Thus, a province's entitlement, E_i, is positive or negative according to whether y_i is smaller or larger than y_c. This formula ensures that there is no net contribution by the federal government. Ideally, a province-to-province equalization formula neutralizes the advantages of living in a province with a high per capita income, or with a large endowment of natural resources, because the post-equalization provincial revenue per head is $t_c y_c$ regardless of the circumstances of the provinces.

With a province-to-province version of the Canadian equalization formula, the entitlement of province i becomes

$$E_i = \sum_{j=1}^{33} t_{cj} \left(Q_{cj} - Q_{ij} \right) P_i \tag{V.3}$$

where Q refers to a provincial tax base per head, the subscript j refers to a tax, and the subscript c refers to the average among provinces. This is the same as the original formula in equation I.4 except that entitlements can now be negative as well as positive, and there is no net contribution from the federal government. The federal government takes from provinces with large tax bases, and gives to provinces with low tax bases. Here, too, there is no advantage in living in a rich or resource-abundant province because equalization ensures that revenue per head is the same in all provinces.

Broadly speaking, a province-to-province equalization formula eliminates one source of inefficiency in provincial taxation and magnifies another. It eliminates the financial incentive of mobile factors of production to migrate from the "have-not" to the "have" provinces, but it magnifies the incentives of the provinces to dicker with their tax structures to increase entitlement to equalization payments. Every province acquires an extra incentive to generate revenue from its deficit tax bases, increasing average provincial tax rates on these bases and driving up its entitlement to equalization payments. Every province acquires an extra incentive to hide as much of its tax base as it can, for each dollar of tax base j that is hidden yields an extra t_{cj} dollars of equalization payment. A province would not be too diligent in tracking down tax evasion. A province would have little incentive to invest in its tax base, for most of the return to the investment would accrue to the rest of Canada. As for provincially-owned resources, provincial politicians would be inclined to give away the tax base to their cronies, for the benefit to their cronies would entail no loss of revenue to the province.

If I own the goose but you have title to the golden eggs, what is it in my interest to do?

To make province-to-province equalization work at all, the federal government would have to specify each province's tax base and, probably, the target average tax rate on each base as well. In effect, the federal government would have to announce each province's equalization tax or equalization entitlement independently of the province's choice of tax rates. Equalization would soon become an enormous source of contention among the provinces and between the provinces and the federal government. This would, of course, constitute a massive violation of Section 125 of the Canadian constitution—that the crown cannot tax the crown—and a giant step away from equity in the sense of rules that all parties can accept.

The province-to-province formula would be a *reductio ad absurdum* of the inclusion within the same constitution of provisions that i) provinces own natural resources, ii) the crown cannot tax the crown and iii) provinces should be able to provide equal services at equal rates of taxation. The three provisions simply do not fit together. Ownership, by its very nature, should convey advantages to the owner; equalization payments would be designed so that it does not. The ordinary equalization formula is a partial retraction by the federal government of the usual rights of ownership. With province-to-province equalization, the dispossession would be complete.

Partial equalization to provinces that are very poor

In view of the uncertainty about the effects of equalization payments on the efficiency of the economy and the distribution of income in the country as a whole, there may be a case for reserving equalization payments for provinces where people are significantly worse off than the average person in the country as a whole. One can be more confident of improving the lot of the poorer members of society when money is directed to provinces that are manifestly poor than when money is directed to all provinces with below average tax bases or incomes per head. Partial equalization can be introduced into the standard Canadian equalization formula or into a macro formula, but a partial macro formula is simpler. To construct such a formula, one must choose a parameter, α, representing the degree of equalization. Necessarily, α is greater than 0 if there is to be any equalization at all, and α is less than 1 when equalization is partial. With partial equalization, the macro formula becomes

$$E_i = \text{the larger of } \{t_c(\alpha y_c - y_i)P_i\ ,0\} \tag{V.4}$$

When the chosen value of α is .85, province i becomes a recipient of equalization payments if and only if its income per head is less than 85 percent of the average income per head in the country as a whole. The macro formula in equation V.4 is identical to the original macro formula in equation V.1 except for the inclusion of the term α. The interpretation of the variables is the same. The formula could be weighted to favour provinces with income per head well below 85 percent of the national average through the use of an artificial tax variable, t_c, which is somewhat larger than the average provincial tax rate.

If Prince Edward Island became gradually more and more prosperous, its entitlement to equalization would gradually diminish under the present formula and under a partial formula as well. The difference is that, under the present formula, payments would continue until the people of Prince Edward Island were as prosperous as the average Canadian, while under a partial formula with α = .85, payments would stop as soon as the people of Prince Edward Island were 85 percent as prosperous as the average Canadian. Similarly, if Ontario became progressively less and less prosperous, equalization payments not would begin under the partial formula until the people of Ontario were only 85 percent as well off as the average Canadian. Total equalization payments by the federal government would, of course, be very much smaller than under the formula in effect today. In judging between the partial formula and the present formula, the central question is who ought to be subsidized under the equalization program, all provinces with less than average tax bases, or provinces that are especially poor? The pros and cons of partial equalization are more or less the same under a macro formula as under the present formula based upon the actual provincial tax base.

The principal effect of replacing of the present equalization formula with a partial formula at a rate of 85 percent would be to eliminate the entitlement of Quebec. At present, the total federal expenditure of about $8 billion on equalization payments is divided more of less equally between Quebec, where there is large population with a small shortfall of income per head, and the Maritimes where there is a small population with a large shortfall of income per head. When α is set at .85, only the latter remains eligible for the program. Views may differ as to whether the identity of the loser in the replacement of one formula by another should be taken into account. Some may argue that if the 85 percent rule, or whatever other rule is being considered, seems reasonable as between Ontario and Prince Edward Island, it ought to remain so no matter whose ox is gored. Others may argue that, as Quebec is different from the other provinces, the special circumstances and character of Quebec ought to be taken into account. But that argument cuts both ways. On the one hand, as Quebec is on the margin of separating from Canada, it may be argued that nothing whatsoever should be done now to worsen the position of Quebec or that may be seen as insulting to Quebec, lest the balance be tipped and Quebec be induced to go. On the other hand, it may be argued that every policy change hurts somebody, and there cannot be a blanket prohibition on policies that happen to hurt Quebec. It may be argued that as Quebec is a distinct society, in fact if not in law, and as Quebec's position in Canada is indeed precarious, the English provinces are and should be less willing to share with Quebec than with one another. The insurance argument for equalization—that the provinces which are at present recipients of equalization may in time become prosperous and supply equalization payments to provinces that are now net contributors to the program—is less applicable to Quebec than to other provinces, because Quebec may no longer be a part of Canada at a time when it would become a contributor to the program.

The financial implications of the present equalization formula, the macro formula, and a partial macro formula with a cut-off of 85 percent of the average gross domestic product per head, are shown in table V.1. In both macro formulas, the average provincial tax rate, t_c, is the ratio of total own-source revenue of the provinces to total Gross Domestic Product. Notice that the Maritimes would benefit from a switch to a

Table V.1: Financial Consequences of Alternative Equalization Formulas, 1994

	(1) Actual Equalization Payments ($ Million)	(2) Equalization Based on Provincial GDP ($ Million)	(3) Equalization Based on 85% of Provincial GDP ($ Million)	(4) Actual Equalization Payment ($ per Head)	(5) Equalization Based on Provincial GDP ($ per Head)	(6) Equalization Based on 85% of GDP ($ per head)
Canada	7,980	6,784	1,114			
Newfoundland	904	834	474	1,553	1,432	814
P.E.I.	170	163	80	1,265	1,213	595
N.S.	869	895	316	928	956	338
N.B.	879	713	244	1,158	940	322
Quebec	3,768	3,106	0	518	427	0
Ontario	0	0	0	0	0	0
Manitoba	867	618	0	767	547	0
Saskatchewan	523	455	0	515	448	0
Alberta	0	0	0	0	0	0
B.C.	0	0	0	0	0	0

Sources: (1) Table I.3, column 3. (2) Computed in accordance with equation V.1. (3) Computed in accordance with equation V.4 where $\alpha=0.85$, and $t_c = 16.08$ percent. The average provincial tax rate is measured as the ratio in 1994 of total provincial own source revenue to total provincial gross domestic product. Total provincial own source income is from *Public Sector Finances*, 1994-1995, Statistics Canada #68-212 Table 1.28. (4) Column 1 divided by column 1 of table I.3. (5) Column 2 divided by column 1 of table I.3. (6) Column 3 divided by column 1 of table I.3.

macro formula, but Quebec would lose. Only the Maritimes would survive as recipients under a partial (85 percent) macro formula.

I conclude this book with a statement of my own preferences for reform. In doing so, I remind the reader that there is no unique, ideally-best design. The effects of a program of equalization payments are so complex, diverse, and, in the end, unpredictable, that the reform of the program is a matter of judgment rather than science. It is a matter of weighing this against that in circumstances where reasonable people differ about relative importance. Furthermore, the evaluation of the program of equalization payments is significantly different for a Canada that includes Quebec than for a separate English Canadian country.

The reason is simple. Because of differences in language, the appropriate scope of the constitutionally-sanctioned powers of the provinces ought to be larger in Canada as it is now than in an entirely English Canadian country. In particular, there would seem to be a strong case in an English Canadian country for reassigning jurisdiction over natural resources and over the redistribution of income from the provincial governments to the federal government. Among the redistributive powers that might be reassigned in an English Canadian country are health care, welfare, and education.

With these powers reassigned to the federal government, the case for equalization payments to assist the poor becomes significantly weaker, if there is anything left of it at all. The connection between poor provinces and poor people would be largely severed, and a greater proportion of the reduced provincial expenditure could be financed by property taxes or other taxes with relatively small effects on the efficiency of the economy as a whole.

There is a dilemma for English Canada in the connection between equalization payments and the allocation of powers between the federal and provincial governments. The case for equalization payments is relatively strong if the powers of the provinces are many, and relatively weak if the powers of the provinces are few. But the greater the powers of the provinces, the more citizens come to identify with their provinces rather than with the nation as a whole, and the less willing the citizens of the rich provinces become to share with the citizens of the poor provinces. A rich resident of a rich province is likely to be more willing to contribute through federal taxation to a national system of welfare for the poor than to finance governments of poor provinces that may or may not reallocate federal transfers to the needy. A poor resident of a rich province is especially reluctant to contribute through federal taxation to the governments of the poor provinces because the ultimate beneficiaries may turn out to be better off than he. This consideration may be important for the evaluation of proposals for the design of a constitution for English Canada in the event of Quebec's separation. It has been suggested that, should Quebec go, a weak federation with limited powers in the federal government would be appropriate. This consideration suggests that a weak federation would be unstable, that it would either evolve into a more centralized state, as the Articles of Confederation were replaced by the American Constitution, or dissolve altogether as provinces opt for full independence or for amalgamation with the United States.

These, in my judgment, are the principal considerations for the evaluation of the options for reform: Though equalization payments may generate a small net transfer to people with incomes per head significantly below the national average, there is also a substantial transfer from rich people in rich provinces to rich people in poor provinces. Dollar for dollar, poor people have far less to gain from equalization payments than from ordinary redistributive expenditure. On balance, there is little reason to suppose that equalization payments contribute to any great extent to the narrowing of the income distribution in the country as a whole. Nor is there a strong case for equalization payments on grounds of efficiency. Anything to be gained from improved allocation among provinces of the mobile factors of production is probably balanced off by the incentives of the provinces to distort their tax structures to increase their entitlement under the program. There is something to the argument that ordinary deadweight loss and interprovincial spillovers in taxation become very large when poor provinces must impose high rates of taxation to provide minimal public services. Local specificity is important for Quebec where language is paramount, but not among the English provinces. The analogy between horizontal equity among people and "equal tax rates for equal public services" among provinces disintegrates on close inspection. The risk of disintegration of society in the violation of horizontal equity within one jurisdiction does not extend across jurisdictions. Once a function of government is placed under provincial jurisdiction, there is no great injustice, and no significant opportunity for victimization when different provinces provide different expenditures per head or impose different rates on similarly-situated taxpayers. The preservation of harmony among people by horizontal equity in taxation within a jurisdiction has no counterpart in taxation among jurisdictions, be they countries or provinces.

For a Canada without Quebec, my first preference is for a unitary state with no constitutionally-sanctioned provinces at all. Jurisdiction over natural resources would be automatically vested in the country as a whole.[23] Redistribution of income, including education and medical care, would automatically be nation-wide. Functions of government may be delegated to municipalities, and there may be transfers from higher to lower levels of government, but there would be no role for anything like the program of equalization payments that is in place today. If there are to be provinces at all, it might be best to deny them jurisdiction over the revenue from natural resources and over the redistribution of income. Federal transfers might then be directed to poor people and equalization payments would be unnecessary.

Federalism should be taken seriously or scrapped. If the provinces are to have jurisdiction over natural resources, it might be best to drop Section 125 of the Constitution and to allow the federal government to tax income accruing in the first instance to the provinces rather than to individuals. There is no benefit in the round about process by which resource-rich provinces are taxed indirectly through the subsidization of other provinces. If Canada is to maintain a program of equalization payments, it might be best to convert to a partial macro formula restricting benefits to provinces that are very poor. This would be less susceptible to manipulation by the provinces and more equalizing on balance than the present formula.

Above all, if Quebec goes, English Canada should take the opportunity to rid itself of Section 36(2). The clause is a time bomb or a deception. It can be a time bomb because the judiciary may one day notice that the present equalization formula does not empower the provinces to supply reasonably comparable levels of public services at reasonably comparable levels of taxation, unless the interpretation of the word reasonably is stretched beyond all reasonable bounds. The Courts may mandate a new formula that is closer to the wording of the constitution but very far from what most citizens desire. Some lawyers claim that Section 36(2) is not "justiciable," but nobody today can bind the Courts tomorrow. If Section 36(2) is really not justiciable, then why, it may be asked, is the clause in the constitution at all? Perhaps the greatest danger is that the federal government may some day try to change the equalization formula and be blocked by the Supreme Court on the grounds that the change is too far from any reasonable interpretation of Section 36(2). The case against a constitutional mandate for equalization payments is essentially the same as the case against a constitutional mandate for particular tax laws. Neither pertains to a fundamental issue of justice on which the legislature is inclined to give way the courts. Both entail a risk of a major constitutional crisis if the courts forbid what the legislature is determined to do.

On the other hand, the clause is a deception unless the practice of equalization conforms in some degree to the wording of the clause. It is in the very nature of a constitution that each clause is deemed worthy to be enforced by the Supreme Court. To constitutionalize equalization payments unenforceably is to hoodwink citizens and, ultimately, to undermine that respect for the constitution on which enforcement of our fundamental rights and of the basic rules of government depends.[24]

For a Canada that includes Quebec, there is a stronger case for equalization payments, but not necessarily to Quebec. The case for equalization rests on the premise that a Canada including Quebec will continue to be a very decentralized federation with provincial jurisdiction over natural resources and a good deal of redistribution of income. For reasons discussed above, I would advocate a partial macro formula at about 85 percent. This would concentrate the federal subsidy upon very poor provinces, leaving other provinces to finance their expenditures with their own tax revenue and costing about half as much as the present program. The one clear principle of equity—that each tub should float on its own bottom—would be compromised as little as possible.

Endnotes

1. Among the more important works on the history, mechanics, and justification of the Canadian program of equalization payments are *Fiscal Federal Federalism in Canada, Report on the Parliamentary Task Force on Federal-Provincial Arrangements*, August 1981; *Financing Confederation: Today and Tomorrow*, Economic Council of Canada, 1982 (Prepared under the direction of David Sewell); and Thomas J. Courchene, *Equalization Payments: Past, Present and Future*, Ontario Economic Council, 1984. Though somewhat out of date, Courchene's book is by far the most complete and comprehensive study of equalization payments. There is an extensive discussion of equalization payments and their connection to other social programs in Robin W. Boadway and Paul A.R. Hobson, *Intergovernmental Fiscal Relations in Canada*, Canadian Tax Foundation, 1993. Every year, the Federal-Provincial Relations Division of the Department of Finance publishes a brief report, entitled *The Equalization Program*, covering the mechanics of the program, recent changes and historical statistics on expenditures. Equalization payments are also discussed in a new book by Courchene, *Social Canada in the Millennium: Reform Imperatives and Restructuring Principles*, C.D. Howe Institute, 1994. For an analysis very different from mine on the place of equalization payments in Canadian federalism, see Robin Boadway, "The Changing Face of Canadian Federalism: The Fiscal Dimension" and "Reforming Social Policy: Can the Federal Government Deliver?" The E.S. Woodward Lectures, The University of British Columbia, 1995.

2. For the property tax, the description of the revenue base in *The Canada Gazette* begins as follows (1993, Part II, Vol. 127, No. 9, 1768-1816):

> (cc) in the case of provincial and local government property taxes, the amount computed in accordance with the formula
> A + B + C
> where
> (i) 'A' is equal to (D + E + F) x G) + H,
> (ii) "B" is equal to (((I + J) x K) + L) x M,
> (iii) "C" is equal to ((N x 0) + P) x Q,
> (iv) "D" is equal to the value of personal disposable income for the calendar year that ends in the preceding fiscal year, less provincial and local indirect taxes for that year, other than provincial and local property taxes, non-profit taxes on corporations, motor vehicle licence and permit fees paid by businesses, miscellaneous taxes on natural resource and provincial and local taxes on the sale price and value of real property on its transfer n each province, as determined by Statistics Canada for the purposes of its annual publication entitled *Provincial Economic Accounts Annual Estimates*,
> (v) "E" is equal to the product obtained when
>
> (A) the population of the province in preceding fiscal year, multiplied by
> (B)
> (1) 0.531581, in the case of Newfoundland,
> (II) 0.396070, in the case of Prince Edward Island,
> (III) 0.662435, in the case of Nova Scotia,
> (IV) 0.473576, in the case of New Brunswick,
> (V) 1.391521, in the case of Quebec,
> (VI) 1.629824, in the case of Ontario,
> (VII) 0.999044, in the case of Manitoba,
> (VIII) 0.622947, in the case of Saskatchewan,
> (IX) 1.076402, in the case of Alberta, and
> (X) 1.712375, in the case of British Columbia,
> is multiplied by
> (B) a fraction, of which the numerator is the aggregate of the amounts determined under subparagraph (iv) for the 10

> provinces, and the denominators is the aggregate of the amounts determined under clause (A) for the 10 provinces.

Nowhere in *The Canada Gazette* is it explained why these numbers are what they are, why, for example, population is multiplied by 1.076402 for Alberta but by 1.712385 for British Columbia. I am confident a rationale can be provided, but none is given in the document or in any publicly-available source that has come to my attention. I would not be surprised to learn that the choice of these numbers over other equally plausible numbers has been hotly contested by provinces that stand to lose or gain significant amounts of money from the final decision. I am not suggesting deception or bad faith. I am asserting that the application of the Canadian formula is more judgmental and more open to dispute than one might at first suppose.

3. Table I.5 is constructed out of the data in appendix table I.2. The column entitled "The Sum of all Expenditures in $1994" is constructed by scaling up current dollar values by the consumer price index and then adding up all the constant dollar values from the beginning of the program to the present. Denote the current value of equalization payments to province i in the year t by $X(i,t)$. The corresponding value in $1994 is denoted by $Y(i,t)$ where

$$Y(i,t) = X(i,t)/[CPI(1994)/CPI(t)]$$

where CPI(t) is shown in the second to last column of appendix table I.2. For each province i, the numbers in the first column of Table I.5 are the sum of $Y(i,t)$ for all t from 1957 to 1994.

The last four columns are computed by iteration. For each province i, the debt equivalents in the year t is $Z(i,t)$ defined as follows: Obviously, $Z(i,1957) = X(i,1957)$ because there is no accumulated debt in the first year of the program. From then on,

$$Z(i,t) = X(i,t) + Z(i,t-1)[1 + r(t)]$$

where r(t) is the postulated rate of interest on the Canadian debt in the year t. The numbers in the four last columns of table I.5 are the values of $Z(i,1994)$ for four postulated values of r(t), the rate on 90-day Treasury Bills, that rate plus 1 percent, that rate plus 2 percent and that rate plus 3 percent.

4. James M. Buchanan, "Federalism and Fiscal Equity," *American Economic Review*, 1950, pp. 583-99. This paper has been the inspiration for a vast literature, some of which is discussed in footnotes to the chapter on efficiency.

5. For a more precise analysis than is contained here, see C.C. Brown and W.E. Oates, "Assistance to the Poor in a Federal System," *Journal of Public Economics*, 1987, 307-30. The paper contains references to earlier literature on the subject. See also, M. Feldstein and M. Vaillant, "Can State Taxes Redistribute Income?" (NBER Working Paper No. 4785).

6. The effect of equalization payments on the provinces' willingness to redistribute income is unlikely to be considerable because equalization payments have "income effects" on provincial spending, but no "substitution effects." The cost to the rich of the redistribution of income to the poor does not diminish relative to the cost of any other item of public expenditure. By contrast, the federal transfer of money to the provinces under the old *Canada Assistance Plan* (covering half of each province's expenditure on welfare) had a substitution effect as well as an income effect, that is to say, the *Canada Assistance Plan* reduced the cost to taxpayers in a province of supplying any given amount of welfare to the poor.

7. The key assumption in the construction of table II.5 is that both province's production functions are Cobb-Douglas. The general form of the production function is

$$Q = K^{(1-\alpha)}L$$

where Q is output, K is land, L is labour and α is a parameter specific to the province ($0 < \alpha < 1$). The wage paid by employers is

$$w = \delta Q/\delta L = \alpha Q/L$$

and the elasticity of the wage with respect to the supply of labour becomes

$(L/w)(\delta w/\delta L) = -(1-\alpha)$

In the construction of the table, the supply of land in each province is assumed fixed, and only labour is variable. The production functions are

$Q_A = 1,000(L_A)^{\frac{1}{2}}$

for province A,

$Q_B = 6,342.5 ln(L_B)^{\frac{1}{4}}$

for province B in case (i), and

$Q_B = 201.8 ln(L_B)^{\frac{3}{4}}$

for province B in case (ii). Thus the elasticity of the wage with respect to the labour force is $-\frac{1}{2}$ in province A, $-\frac{3}{4}$ in province B for case (i) and $-\frac{1}{4}$ in province B for case (ii).

With no transfer of income to workers to workers in either province, the wages in the two provinces, w_A and w_B, must be the same. With a transfer of $1,000 to each worker in province B and with costless mobility of labour, the relation between the wages becomes

$w_A = w_B + 1,000/L_B$

from which all the numbers in the table can be determined.

A similar procedure is adopted in table III.1. With 100 landowners in province A, 300 landowners in province B, 200 workers altogether (so that $L_A + L_B = 200$), $4,000 of oil revenue in province A, an equalization payment of $2,500 from the federal government to province B and free mobility of labour between the provinces, the relation between wages in the two provinces becomes

$w_A + 4,000/(100 + L_A) = w_B + 2,500/(500 - L_A)$

The last expression in this equation vanishes in the absence of equalization payments.

8. The modern literature on the efficiency of equalization payments can be seen as a response to Anthony D. Scott's assertion in "A Note on grants in Federal Countries" (*Economica*, 1950, 416-22) that

> transfers to poor people in resource-poor states . . . may undesirable in the long run for the following reason: the maximization of income for the whole country [is] to be achieved only . . . when resources and labour are combined in such a way that marginal products of similar units of labour is the same in all places. . . . [T]ransfers of income from place to place counteract this incentive to labour mobility and thus prevent the maximization of national production (419).

Other economists then sought to discover reasons why marginal products of similar units of labour in different provinces might not be the same in the absence of equalization payments. In two important papers, James M. Buchanan and Richard E. Wagner, "An Efficiency Basis for Federal Fiscal Equalization," in Julius Margolis, ed. *The Analysis of Public Output*, 1970, and James M. Buchanan and Charles J. Goetz, "Efficiency Limits to Fiscal Mobility," *Journal of Public Economics*, 1972, pp. 25-43, Buchanan and his co-authors argued that, in the words of the latter paper, a federation without equalization payments and where labour is mobile among provinces "is likely to lead to overconcentration of population in those communities where public-goods quantities are large. This would, in turn, suggest that there may be an overconcentration of persons in the larger communities and in communities with higher than average income levels" (33). The latter paper is, to my knowledge the first to make explicit use of variants of equations III.1 and III.2 in the text. For an early and quite insightful discussion of the economics of the Canadian program, see John F. Graham, "Fiscal Adjustment in a Federal Country," in *Intergovernmental Fiscal Relations*, Canadian Tax Papers #40, Canadian Tax Foundation, 1964.

A more analytically satisfying derivation of optimal subsidies from the federal government to selected provinces is contained in Frank Flatters, Vernon Henderson, and Peter Mieszkowski, "Public Goods, Efficiency and Regional Equalization," *Journal of Public Economics*, 1974, pp. 99-112. An explicit basis in efficiency for the Canadian program of equalization payments is provided in Robin W. Boadway and Frank Flatters, "Efficiency and Equalization Payments in a Federal System of Government," *Canadian Journal of*

Economics, 1982, pp. 613-33, which has had a great deal of influence on how Canadians think about equalization payments. In this paper, identical workers allocate themselves between two provinces, each of which supplies the optimal amount of pure (province-wide) public goods in an otherwise undistorted economy where second best considerations are assumed away. It is shown that there is an optimal transfer of income between provinces, but it is not established that the optimal transfer is necessarily from the rich province to the poor province and there is no attempt to estimate the magnitude of the gain from the establishment of the optimal equalization payment.

Subsequently, it was demonstrated by Gordon Myers in "Optimality, Free Mobility and Regional Authority in a Federation," *Journal of Public Economics*, 1990, pp. 107-121 that, with complete mobility of labour, and if every person owns an equal share of the land in every province, efficient transfers of income among provinces would be made voluntarily by the provincial governments. In "Rent Seeking and Tax Competition," *The Journal of Public Economics*, forthcoming, Sam Bucovetsky shows that, if landowners in each province are distinct groups, then inter-provincial transfers would not be made voluntarily by the provinces, and it would be efficient for the federal government to transfer income to the "have" rather than to the "have not" provinces. See also John B. Burbidge and Gordon M. Meyers, "Redistribution within and across Regions of a Federation," *Canadian Journal of Economics*, 1994, pp. 620-36 and David E. Wildasin, "Income Redistribution and Migration," *Canadian Journal of Economics*, 1994, pp. 637-56.

9. The story is illustrated in figure 1 for a country with two provinces, A and B. In each province, labour is combined with land to produce grain. The core of the land-labour distinction is that labour is completely mobile between provinces, while land is completely immobile. Labour is shown on the horizontal axis, the marginal product of labour in province A is shown in the left hand vertical axis, and the marginal product of labour in province B is shown on the right hand vertical axis, where the marginal product of labour in a province is defined as the increase in the output of grain from the addition of one extra worker to the province. The total supply

Figure 1

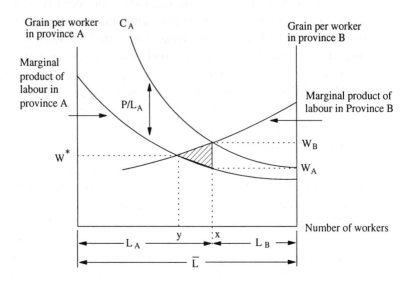

of labour, $\overline{L}$, is the distance between the right and left hand vertical axes. The number of workers, L_A, in province A is a distance to the right of the left hand vertical axis. The number of workers, L_B, in province B is a distance to the left of the right hand vertical axis. The two principal curves in the figure show the dependence in each province of the marginal product of labour upon the supply of labour. These marginal product of labour curves are downward sloping—from left to right for province A and from right to left for province B—to reflect the diminishing marginal product of labour in the production of grain; the larger the labour force in a province, the less extra grain does each extra worker produce.

Competition among landowners for labour ensures that the wage of labour in each province is equal to the marginal product of labour. Mobility of labour between provinces ensures that the net incomes of workers are the same in both provinces. Net incomes must be the same, for, otherwise, the entire labour force would locate in the province with the higher wage. In the absence of taxes and transfers, the wages of workers in both provinces must be the same as well.

Total output of grain in the country as a whole depends on how the total supply of labour is allocated between the provinces. By construction, the output of grain in each province is the area under its marginal product of labour curve, over the distance L_A for province A and over the distance L_B for province B. Thus, the efficient allocation of labour between the provinces, that for which total output of grain in the country as a whole is maximized, is identified by the crossing of the two marginal product of labour curves above the point y on the horizontal axis. When labour is allocated efficiently, the common marginal product of labour is w^*.

If, instead, the allocation of labour were as indicated by the point x, with more workers an province A and less in province B, the marginal product of labour, w_A, in province A would be less than the marginal product of labour, w_B, in province B. In that case, the migration of one worker from province A to province B would decrease output in province A by less than the increase in output in province B, and there would be an increase of $w_B - w_A$ in the output in the country as a whole. When the allocation of labour is inefficient as indicated by the point x, the national income is less than it might be by an amount represented by the area of the shaded triangle.

Now suppose that the total income of labour is augmented by oil rent, and let P be the total value (in units of grain) of the rent accruing to labour. If the oil rent is owned nationally and allocated equally to all workers, the income of workers in both provinces is increased by an amount $P/\overline{L}$, but no incentive is created for workers to migrate from one province to another. By contrast, if the oil rent is owned by province A and allocated equally among all workers in that province, then each worker in province A receives an amount P/L_A, while workers in province B receive nothing. Thus, the income per worker in province B is just equal to his wage w_B, while the income per worker in province A is the sum, $w_A + P/L_A$, of his wage and his transfer from the province made possible by the province's oil revenue.

In these circumstances, the equilibrium allocation of labour between the provinces is at the crossing of the marginal product of labour curve in province B and the curve C_A, which is the marginal product of labour curve in province A raised for each value of L_A by an amount P/L_A. As is evident from inspection of the figure, the new equilibrium condition is $w_B = w_A + P/L_A$, which can only hold when there is an inefficiently large number of workers in province A. It is evident from inspection of the figure that efficiency could be restored by an appropriately large equalization payment from the federal government to province B; the incomes of workers in both provinces would be reduced by the federal tax required to finance the equalization payment, the income in province B would be increased by the equalization payment and labour would reallocate itself efficiently.

10 In "An Estimate of the Welfare Gain from Fiscal Equalization," *Canadian Journal of Economics*, 1986, pp. 298-308, William G. Watson argued that gains to equalization-induced mobility of labour are likely to be very small. That is not surprising, for estimates of static welfare loss are almost always small. (Suppose, for example, that there are 10 million people in the recipient provinces and that equalization payments of $600 per person—$6 billion in total—inhibit the migration of 1 percent of the population of the recipient provinces, approximately 100,000 people. Applying the usual formula for deadweight loss on the assumption that the allocation of labour among provinces is efficient once the program of equalization payments is in place, the net gain from the program for the country as a whole would be $\frac{1}{2}\Delta P \Delta Q$ where ΔP is $600 and ΔQ is 100,000. The gain would be $30 million, about half the cost of the new library at Queen's University or one two-hundredth of the transfer of income under the program.)

11. The efficiency argument for equalization payments in endnote 9 rests on two premises: i) that the allocation of labour between the provinces would be inefficient in the absence of equalization payments, and ii) that the inefficiency is such that there would be too few workers in the recipient provinces and too many workers in the

Figure 2

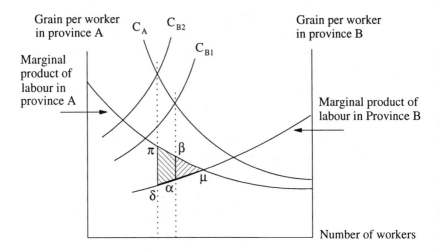

other provinces. The first premise is innocuous because the world is always somewhat inefficient for one reason or another. The second premise is crucial. The second premise is valid in the example in endnote 9 where provincially-owned oil revenue is the only source of the misallocation of labour. It may not be valid in practice. Unemployment insurance, welfare or pure inertia could be impeding the movement of people from provinces where the marginal product of labour is low to provinces where the marginal product of labour is higher, and, if that were so, equalization payments might magnify rather than reduce the loss of output of grain from the inappropriate allocation of labour.

Figure 2 is a reproduction of the figure 1 in endnote 9 together with two new curves, the curve C_{B1} showing the income per worker inclusive of transfers in province B in the absence of a program of equalization payments, and the curve C_{B2} showing the income per worker inclusive of transfers in province B when equalization payments are provided. Think of the gap between C_{B1} and the marginal product of labour curve for province B as representing the net transfer per worker (payments from the province less taxes to the province) in province B. If, as may well be the case, this gap exceeds the comparable gap between C_A and the marginal product of labour curve in province A, then, in the absence of equalization payments, there would be too many workers in province B, with a loss of output of $\alpha\beta\mu$. But province B may still be the "have not" province and the recipient of equalization payments. In that case, the effect of the program of equalization payments would be to raise the income of labour curve in province B from C_{B1} to C_{B2} and to magnify the loss of output of grain from the misallocation of labour between the provinces from $\alpha\beta\mu$ to $\pi\delta\mu$, so that the total output decreases by an amount represented by the area $\alpha\beta\delta\pi$. The program of equalization payments would be clearly inefficient in this case. (The reader who finds this analysis somewhat artificial, even phoney, should bear in mind that it is the basis of the standard and often-repeated efficiency argument for equalization payments and that my purpose here is to dismiss the argument as empirically unsupported and theoretically inconclusive.)

12. The taxpayer's manoeuvres to escape taxation have three marked consequences for the government's capacity to raise revenue by taxation: the full cost of taxation to the taxpayer exceeds the value of the revenue obtained, the ratio of full cost to revenue is an increasing function of the rate of tax, and there is typically a maximum rate beyond which an increase in the rate raises the cost of taxation to the taxpayer without generating any extra revenue at all.

These propositions can be illustrated in a simple example. Consider the taxation of water from a publicly-owned well with unlimited capacity. Since the capacity of the well is unlimited and since the only cost of water to consumers is the tax imposed by the government, the tax on water and the price of water are one and the same. Suppose the community's demand curve for water is a downward-sloping straight line.

$$q = \bar{q}[1 - t/\bar{p}]$$

where t is the tax per gallon, q is the number of gallons consumed, and $\bar{q}$ and $\bar{p}$ are parameters to be interpreted respectively as the amount of water people would draw from the well if water were free and the price at which the demand for water falls to zero. The demand curve is illustrated in figure 3, with price on the vertical axis, quantity on the horizontal axis and intersections $\bar{p}$ and $\bar{q}$.

When the tax rate is t, the revenue, R(t), from the tax is

$$R = tq = t\bar{q}[1 - (t/\bar{p})] = \bar{q}[t - (t^2/\bar{p})]$$

Increase the tax rate slightly from t to t+Δt. The corresponding change in revenue is

$$\Delta R \equiv R(t + \Delta t) - R(t) = \bar{q}[1 - 2t/\bar{p}]\Delta t - (\bar{q}/\bar{p})\Delta t^2$$

where the final expression can be ignored because Δt^2 becomes *very* small when Δt is small, so that

$$\Delta R = \bar{q}[1 - 2t/\bar{p}]\Delta t$$

Starting from a situation where water is untaxed, the introduction of a small tax Δt yields a revenue of qΔt. Then, every extra increase Δt yields a progressively smaller extra revenue, until, when the tax rises to $\bar{p}/2$, there is no extra revenue at all. The relation between tax revenue and tax rate is shown in figure 4.

There is a parallel story about the cost of taxation to the taxpayer. Starting from any given tax t (as long as t is less than $\bar{p}/2$), an increase in the tax from t to t+Δt imposes two costs on the taxpayer. The first cost is the tax itself, the loss to the taxpayer of the goods and services other than water he must give up to pay to extra tax. This cost ΔR. The second cost is the loss to the taxpayer of the water he is deterred from taking because of the rise in the tax. He is deterred even though his tax-induced abstinence imposes no cost on anybody else. This cost is tΔq, the product of amount of water he desists from taking and the value of water per gallon, which is just equal to the tax.

Thus, the ratio, S, of "the extra cost of the tax to the taxpayer" to the "extra revenue acquired" from a small increase in the tax is

$$S = (\Delta R + t\Delta q)/(\Delta R)$$

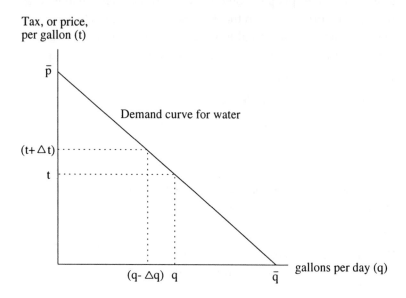

**Figure 3: How the demand for water
varies with the rate of tax**

Figure 4: How revenue varies with the rate of tax

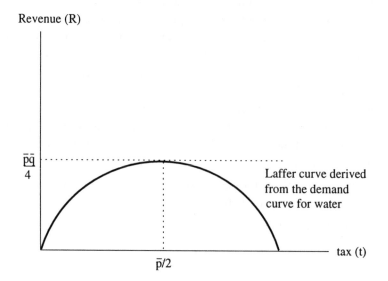

Figure 5: How the cost to taxpayers,
per dollar of tax, varies with the tax rate

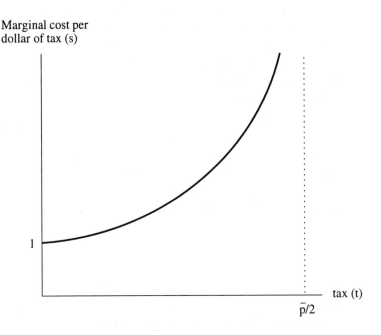

Marginal cost per
dollar of tax (s)

1

tax (t)

$\bar{p}/2$

From the demand curve above, it follows immediately that the change, Δq, in the quantity of water consumed resulting from a small increase, Δt, in the tax rate is

$$\Delta q \equiv \bar{q}[1 - (t + \Delta t)p] - \bar{q}[1 - t/p] = -(\bar{q}/p)\Delta t$$

Thus,

$$S = \{\bar{q}[1 - (2t/\bar{p})]\Delta t + t(\bar{q}/\bar{p})\Delta t\} / \{\bar{q}[1 - (2t/\bar{p}]\Delta t\}$$

$$= (\bar{p} - t)/(\bar{p} - 2t)$$

This ratio is equal to 1 when $t = 0$ because water is free and therefore worthless at the margin when there is no tax. It increases steadily with t, rising to infinity as t approaches $\bar{p}/2$ because, at $t = \bar{P}/2$, an increase in tax would still deter some consumption of water but would yield no extra revenue. The gradual rise in the full cost of taxation to the taxpayer per unit of extra revenue—from $S = 1$ when $t = 0$ to $s =$ infinity when $t = \bar{p}/2$—is illustrated in figure 5.

The example is considerably more general than it may at first appear. One way or another, tax bases shrink as tax rates increase because taxpayers adjust their behaviour to reduce liability for tax. As long as there is a rate of tax, comparable to $\bar{p}$ in the example, high enough to eliminate purchase of taxed items altogether, there is a somewhat lower "maximal" tax rate at which revenue is maximized, and the ratio of the burden on the taxpayer to the amount of revenue raised from an increase in the tax rate must rise to infinity as that maximal rate is approached.

For a general discussion of the measurement of deadweight loss, see Dan Usher, "The Hidden Costs of Public Expenditure," in Richard M. Bird (ed.), *More Taxing than Taxes? The Tax-like Effects of Nontax Policies in LDCs*, ICS Press, 1991. On deadweight loss in federal government, see R. H. Gordon, "An Optimal Taxation Approach to Fiscal Federalism," *Quarterly Journal of Economics*, 1983, pp. 567-86, and D.E. Wildasin, *Urban Public Finance*, 1986, chapter 5.

13. In "Fiscal Capacity, Tax Effort and Optimal Equalization Grants," *Canadian Journal of Economics*, 1994, pp. 657-72, B. Dahlby and L.S. Wilson construct a model in which equalization payments generate an increase in the national income because, without equalization payments, the marginal cost of public funds would be higher in poor provinces than in rich provinces. A province's optimal set of tax rates is that which minimizes the total excess burden in the province as a whole. That, in turn is achieved when the marginal social cost of taxation, the height of the curve S in figure 5 of footnote 12, is the same for all taxes. It is customary in the literature of fiscal federalism to refer to a province's fiscal capacity. The only sensible meaning I can attach to the term "fiscal capacity" is the revenue attained at "maximal" rates for all taxes. Conceivably, the cost to a province of maintaining national standards could exceed its fiscal capacity in this sense of the term.

14. The classic on this topic is Thomas J. Courchene, and David A. Beavis, "Federal-Provincial Tax Equalization: An Evaluation," *Canadian Journal of Economics*, 1973, pp. 483-502. Courchene returned

to the topic in an appendix (with David Wildasin) to *Equalization Payments: Past, Present and Future*, Ontario Economic Council, 1984. See also Richard A. Musgrave, "Approaches to a Fiscal Theory of Political Federalism," in *Public Finances: Needs, Sources and Utilization*, 1961.

15. There are odd and unexpected consequences of the loss to the recipient province of the incentive to preserve its tax base. Here are two examples. The equalization program may have saved Quebec from the adverse financial consequences of its language policy. Tom Courchene has pointed out that, in 1978, "for each additional percentage point that Quebec's share of Canada's population exceeds its share of the income base, federal equalization payments will increase by approximately $75 million. This reduces substantially the cost to the Quebec economy of a wholesale out-flow of non-French speaking Quebeckers, assuming that they are in the top half of Quebec's income distribution. Put more bluntly, the structure of federal transfers is such as to lend incentives to the Parti Quebecois to come down harder on the English Quebecker, than would be the case if Quebec were an independent nation." ("Avenues of Adjustment: The Transfer System and Regional Disparities," *Canadian Confederation at the Crossroads*, Vancouver: The Fraser Institute, 1978, p. 163.)

A second anomaly in the equalization program, also noticed by Tom Courchene, is that the recent federal cutback of transfer payments to Ontario hit the residents of Ontario twice, once directly as provincial tax rates in Ontario increase to make up the lost revenue, and again indirectly because the residents of Ontario pay the lion's share of the increase in federal taxation to cover the increase in equalization payments warranted as a consequence of the increase across Canada in provincial tax rates. The cutback in federal transfers to the provinces in the current (1995) budget is expected to increase equalization payments from $8 billion to about $9.3 billion.

16. *New Estimates, Department of Finance, 1994-95.*

17. "Federalism and Fiscal Equity," *American Economic Review*, 1950, 583-99, p. 592.

18. In the most mischievous and confusing terminology in the entire lexicon of economics, Richard Musgrave (*The Theory of Public Finance*, 1959, p. 160) distinguished, as "different sides of the same coin," between horizontal and vertical equity, the one a "safeguard against capricious discrimination" and the other a synonym for equality. The difficulty with this terminology is not just that the messy and highfalutin term "vertical equity" has replaced a perfectly serviceable word, "equality." It is that scholars have started referring to "equality" as "equity" without the qualifier. The expression "horizontal equity" has become too closely bound to characteristics of the income tax, and the broader meaning of the word "equity" is lost altogether. It has become difficult to use the word "equity" in its meaning in common speech because the word has been hijacked for another usage altogether. I revert to common usage none the less.

19. The distinction between source-based and person-based revenues of the provincial governments is discussed extensively by Robin Boadway and Frank Flatters in *Equalization in a Federal State: An Economic Analysis*, Economic Council of Canada, 1982.

20. F.R. Scott, "The Constitutional Background of Taxation Agreements," *McGill Law Journal*, 1955, pp. 1-10.

21. It is difficult, bordering on impossible, for an outsider to the federal-provincial negotiations to get to the bottom of this question. Gordon Gibson, who has played a significant role in the government of British Columbia, has this to say:

> Equalization could be one of the noblest of Canadian concepts, were it devoted to ensuring that all young Canadians, who cannot control where they live, have an equal start in life. It becomes an important philosophical debate as to whether the concept should be extended further than that,

and a bit of a scandal when elements of the pork barrel enter into setting the numbers. As any provincial Minister of Finance will tell you, the Feds set the result first and then jigger the extremely complex formula to make the desired numbers happen for the chosen political objectives. (*Plan B: The Future of the Rest of Canada*, Vancouer: The Fraser Institute, 1994, p. 63.)

We are informed by the Department of Finance in *The Equalization Program*, April, 1994, p. 11, that "renewals of equalization do not involve intergovernmental negotiations but have been preceded in each case by extensive consultations between the federal government and the ten provinces." The "floors," the "ceilings," and the "tax-back" provisions, to be discussed below in the text, introduce an arbitrariness into the entitlements of the provinces. These provisions may be justified on some principle of good government, or they may be arranged "to make the desired numbers happen," or both. Tom Courchene notes that Nova Scotia's off-shore oil revenue is to be sheltered from equalization; he deplores this, fearing that "equalization will cease to be formula-based, and it could well degenerate into a program determined principally by political and paternalistic considerations." (*Equalization Payments: Past, Present and Future*, p. 401.)

22. For a detailed examination of proposals for the reform of the Canadian program of equalization payments, see "Options Forgone," part V of Courchene's *Equalization Payments: Past, Present and Future*. This contains discussions of the history and analytics of the macro formula and of proposals for the total or partial sharing of resource revenue. What I call partial formulas are not discussed.

23. I have tried to develop the case for a unitary state in "The Interests of English Canada" (with comments by William Watson and a reply) in the March 1995 issue of *Canadian Public Policy*. For the opposite view that English Canada would be best served by a radical devolution of jurisdiction to the provinces, see *Plan B* by Gordon Gibson (cited in note 17 above). Gibson and I cross swords

briefly in the March 1995 issue of the *Atlantic Economic Review*.

24. Lawyers have claimed that Section 36(2) is not justiciable, that it is no more than a vague expression of intent that binds the federal government to nothing. The tip-off is the phrase "are committed to the principle."

Appendix Table 1: Summary of 33 Revenue Sources and Revenue Bases Contained in the Fiscal Equalization Program for 1982 to 1987, with changes since 1987 added in square brackets at the end of some sections

Revenue Source	Revenue Base
1) Personal income taxes	Simulated yield in each province of the representative provincial personal income tax. This yield is determined through the Revenue Canada Personal Income Tax Microsimulation Model (PITAX), which is used to calculate for each federal personal income tax bracket the effective average rate of tax for the 10 provinces in relation to federal basic tax. (The resulting rates reflect the various provincial tax credits, surtaxes, and tax cuts and the various features of the Quebec tax system.) The simulate yield is obtained for each province and each tax bracket by multiplying the average rate for a bracket by the portion of the province's federal basic tax falling within the bracket. The total simulated yields of the provinces are determined by summing their yields for each tax bracket, and by adjusting the resulting totals to take account of differences among provinces in the proportion of total tax returns assessed as of the cutoff date for the purposes of inclusion in the tax model.
2) Revenues from business income: a) corporate income tax; b) remittances of provincial government business enterprises other than liquor commissions, lotteries, and the B.C. Petroleum Corporation; and c) shared revenues under the Public Utilities Income Transfer Act	Private business profits before losses (national accounts total, distributed by province on the basis of how corporate taxable income is allocated) plus provincial government business enterprise profits of profit-making corporations other than liquor commissions, lottery enterprises, and B.C. Petroleum Corporation (distributed by province on a national accounts basis). Corporate taxable income excludes estimated income arising from the non-expensing of provincial levies on oil and on gas. The latter equals oil and gas royalties and other special levies on oil and gas to the extent that they exceed the federal 25 percent resource allow-

Appendix table 1 continued

Revenue Source	Revenue Base

<table>
<tr><td></td><td>ance in respect of oil and gas. There is a special reduced weight for that portion of corporate taxable income that is eligible for the small business tax rate to take account of the lower rate that is typically imposed by provinces on such income.</td></tr>
<tr><td>3) Tax on corporate capital</td><td>Value of those elements of corporate capital that are typically included in the base of taxes on capital by those provinces that levy such a tax. The tax base generally includes equity capital, various reserves, long-term debt, and some short-term debt. Equity capital consists of the paid-up value of common and preferred shares, retained earnings, contributed surplus, and other surplus. Reserves include most reserves that are not deductible for income tax purposes. Debt includes all secured debt, all debt to other corporations, and debt to shareholders. Certain adjustments are made in respect of accumulated capital consumption allowances and investment in other corporations. Banks and trust and loan companies are subject to special treatment in the tax base because these institutions are taxed by the provinces in a manner that differs from that applied to other corporations. Accordingly, the portion of the tax base for banks and trust and loan companies is limited to equity capital, but this portion of the base is given a special weight of 2.5, which reflects the higher rate of tax typically applied to these institutions by the provinces. [Revenues now include debt guarantee fees. Paid-up capital is allocation by *assets* by sector.]</td></tr>
<tr><td>4) General and miscellaneous sales taxes</td><td>Value of retail sales in the province (excluding food, children's clothing and footwear, tobacco, and motive fuel), plus cost, net of provincial sales tax, of materials used in construction, plus capital and repaid expenditures for investment in place</td></tr>
</table>

Appendix table 1 continued

Revenue Source	Revenue Base
	for machinery and equipment (excluding agriculture and fishing), plus sales of hotel, motel, tourist court, telephone, theatre, and cablevision services, plus receipts of restaurants, caterers, and taverns. [The tax base now includes tobacco and excludes prescription drugs as well as investment in machinery and equipment for all primary industries, the manufacturing sector and the government sector.]
5) Tobacco taxes	Number of cigarettes (or equivalent re cigars and tobacco) sold in each province.
6) Gasoline taxes, including aviation fuel	Number of litres of gasoline sold in province with differential weights for gasoline for (1) road use by non-farm vehicles, (2) road use by farm vehicles, and (3) use by aircraft—with the different weights reflecting the average levels of taxation typically imposed by the 10 provinces on each category for the calendar year.
7) Diesel fuel taxes, including railway fuel	Number of litres of diesel fuel sold in province with differential weights for diesel fuel sold for: (1) road use by non-farm vehicles, (2) road use by farm vehicles, and (3) use by railway locomotives—with the different weights reflecting the average level of taxation typically imposed by the 10 provinces on each category for the calendar year.
8) Motor vehicle licence revenue, non-commercial	Total number of passenger vehicle registrations in the province, with motorcycles and mopeds given a commercial weighting of 0.40.
9) Motor vehicle licence revenue, commercial	Total value of sales of commercial vehicles in the province for the current and previous five years in constant dollars.
10) Alcohol—spirits	Volume of spirits sold in the province.

Appendix table 1 continued

Revenue Source	Revenue Base
11) Alcohol—wine	Volume of wine sold in the province.
12) Alcohol—beer	Volume of beer sold in the province. [Items 10, 11 and 12 are now combined in a single revenue-weighted base.]
13) Hospital and medical care insurance	Estimated number of persons in respect of whom premiums would be levied in a province on the basis of the typical tax structure in those provinces that levy premiums. Estimate based on the number of federal income tax returns filed by persons under the age of 65 resident in the province with taxable income large enough for premium to apply. Separate taxable income thresholds established for persons taxed as married and single and for persons within each of these two categories that are typically eligible for 25, 50 and 75 percent exemptions from premiums in the premium-levying provinces.
14) Succession duties and gift taxes	Estimate, from federal income tax returns, of the total income of "high-income persons" in each province with special high weights for persons 65 and over to reflect their relatively high mortality rates. "High-income persons" are defined as those who have an income of $90,000 or over—based on the "total income" from federal income tax returns, adjusted to include capital gains in full and to exclude the gross-up of dividend income. [Discontinued]
15) Race track taxes	Amounts wagered in the province at parimutuel tracks on harness and running horse races.
16) Forestry revenues	Value added for the forest industry from Crown lands in the province. [Value added replaced by volume.]

Appendix table 1 continued

Revenue Source	Revenue Base
17) Conventional new oil revenues, including conventional NORP oil (consists mainly of royalties)	Value of production of conventional new oil within the province from Crown and freehold lands. Separate determination made for conventional NORP oil (which is effectively treated as a separate revenue source) to reflect the relatively high rate of taxation that is typically imposed on this category of conventional new oil. A special adjustment is made to the tax base in respect of freehold production to reflect the generally lower rates of tax applied to such production. [Base excludes heavy oil. NORP has been discontinued].
18) Conventional old oil revenues (consists mainly of royalties)	Value of production of conventional old oil within the province from Crown and freehold lands. A special adjustment is made to the tax base in respect of freehold production to reflect the generally lower rates of tax applied to such production. [Base excludes heavy oil.]
19) Heavy oil, including NORP oil conventional new oil, and conventional old oil but excluding Cold Lake production (consists mainly of royalties and of federal revenues from the oil export charge that are shared with provinces)	Value of production of heavy oil within the province from Crown and freehold lands. Heavy oil is defined as NORP oil, conventional new oil, and conventional old oil having a density of $935 \, \mathrm{kg/m^3}$ or more. However, it excludes Cold Lake production. A special adjustment is made to the tax base in respect of freehold production to reflect the generally lower rates of tax applied to such production. [No longer includes NORP oil.]
20) Mined oil, including synthetic oil produced from oil sands (tar sands), and heavy oil produced at Cold Lake, Alberta.	Value of production of synthetic petroleum and Cold Lake heavy oil within the province from Crown and freehold lands. (Cold Lake heavy oil is included in the tax base because it is exceptionally heavy and subject to a special royalty akin to that for synthetic oil.)

Appendix table 1 continued

Revenue Source	Revenue Base
21) Domestic natural gas, including pentanes, propanes, ethanes, butanes, and elemental sulphur (consists mainly of royalties)	Volume of production within the province from Crown and freehold lands for domestic use. [Adjustment to the tax base for freehold production.]
22) Export of natural gas (consists mainly of royalties and remittances to the B.C. government by the B.C. Petroleum Corporation)	Volume of production within the province from Crown and freehold lands for export. [Adjustment to the tax base for freehold production.]
23) Sale of Crown leases of oil and natural gas lands.	Actual revenues of the province from this revenue source in the fiscal year. [Revenue has been replaced by weighted average fiscal capacity of new oil, heavy oil and natural gas.]
24) Other oil and natural gas revenues	Volume of production of oil and natural gas from Crown and freehold lands in the province, with the two components combined on the basis of their energy equivalent values—that is, 1,033 cubic metres of natural gas equalling 1 cubic metre of oil. (Natural gas volumes are determined with respect to unprocessed gas to take account of natural gas liquids.)
25) Metallic and non-metallic minerals other than potash	Value of production of minerals in the province—with separate determinations for five categories of mineral: (1) iron, (2) uranium, (3) asbestos, (4) coal, and (5) residual minerals. Each of these sources is treated as if it were a separate revenue source. The residual category excludes oil, natural gas, elemental sulphur, and potash because revenues from these minerals are equalized under other revenue sources. It also excludes clay products because these are normally assigned to the manufacturing sector. Structural materials other than

Appendix table 1 continued

Revenue Source	Revenue Base
	clay products are included at a reduced weight because of the relatively low resource rents associated with them. [Iron and uranium no longer have separate determinations. They are included in residual minerals.]
26) Potash (includes royalties, but not remittances to the Saskatchewan government by the Saskatchewan Potash Corporation)	Value added by the potash industry in the province. [Value added replaced by volume of production.]
27) Water power rentals	Number of kilowatt hours of electricity generated in the province from publicly and privately owned hydro sources. The tax bases for Newfoundland and Quebec are determined in a special manner by means of two steps. In the first step a combined tax base for Newfoundland and Quebec is determined on the basis of the number of kilowatt hours of electricity generated in the two provinces from publicly and privately owned sources. In the second step the total tax base for Newfoundland and Quebec determined in the first step is allocated between the two provinces in accordance with their relative shares of gross revenues from the sale of all electricity generated within the two provinces by hydro sources. [The fiscal capacity of Churchill Falls attributed to Quebec not Newfoundland.]
28) Insurance premium taxes	Total value of insurance premiums for property and casualty insurance and for life insurance, issued by federally or provincially registered corporations, plus the value of premiums, contributions, and dues of fraternal benefit societies, minus (1) the value of dividends paid to policy holders and (2) marine insurance premiums.

Appendix table 1 continued

Revenue Source	Revenue Base
29) Payroll taxes	Wage and salaries portion of personal income in the province, plus military pay and allowances, but excluding supplementary labour income.
30) Property taxes (includes taxes levied by municipalities, school authorities, and provinces)	Composite base with separate components for the building and land portions of the real property tax base. *Building Component* (70 percent of total base for 10 provinces as a whole) Two subcomponents with equal weight for the 10 provinces as a whole: 1) value of the residential net capital stock in the province, measured in constant 1971 dollars as of the end of the calendar year preceding the fiscal year, and 2) value of that portion of non-residential net capital stock in the province consisting of building construction in all industries other than local government, universities, hospitals, churches, and other institutions, measured in constant 1971 dollars as of the end of the calendar year preceding the fiscal year. *Land Component* (30 percent of total base for 10 provinces as a whole) Net provincial income at factor cost for the calendar year ending in the preceding fiscal year and for the four preceding calendar years in constant dollars. The net provincial income at factor cost for each year is adjusted for the federal tax transfer system. This is done by adding federal transfers to persons in each province and by subtracting a portion of federal direct tax withdrawals from taxpayers in each province. The portion of tax withdrawals that is subtracted is established in such a manner that *for the 10 provinces* the total deductions will exactly equal the amount added in respect of transfer payments. [The tax base has

Appendix table 1 continued

Revenue Source	Revenue Base
	changed completely. Now the base has three sectors—farm, residential and commercial—with building and land components in each.]
31) Lotteries	Personal income excluding: 1) value of change in farm inventory; 2) provincial-local transfers to persons; and 3) federal direct tax withdrawals, consisting of federal income tax on persons (adjusted in the case of Quebec to add back the value of 16.5 point abatement) plus employer and employee contributions to unemployment insurance, the CPP, and the QPP. [The base has changed completely to sales of lottery tickets.]
32) Other taxes and revenues from own sources (miscellaneous revenues from sources such as land transfer taxes, on sales of liquid petroleum gases, crop insurance premiums, fish and game licences, provincial revenues from concessions and franchises, provincial revenues from licences and permits not elsewhere specified, provincial and local government revenues from sales of goods and services, provincial revenues from fines, etc.)	Composite tax base consisting of a weighted average of the tax bases for all revenue sources other than those revenue sources relating specifically to natural resource revenues.

Appendix table 1 continued

Revenue Source	Revenue Base
33) Federal revenues from taxation or natural resources levies, not elsewhere specified, that are shared with provinces on a point-of-origin basis: a) shared tax on the payout of undistributed corporate surplus; and b) shared revenue from offshore minerals.	Actual revenues of the province of each such source in the fiscal year. [Undistributed corporate surplus has been dropped, and preferred share dividends has been added.]

Note: Revenues are measured on the fiscal-year basis for all revenue sources. Revenue bases are usually measured on a calendar-year basis—using the calendar year ending in the fiscal year in which the revenues are derived. A very high proportion of all data inputs for final determinations of equalization entitlements are supplied by the chief statistician of Statistics Canada.

Source: Department of Finance. From Boadway, R.W. and Hobson, P. *Intergovernmental Fiscal Relations in Canada*, National Tax Foundation, Canadian Tax Paper #96, 1993, updated with additional information from the Department of Finance.

Appendix Table 2: Equalization Payments, (millions of current dollars)

Year	Nfld.	P.E.I.	N.S.	N.B.	Que.	Man.	Sask.	Alta.	B.C.	Cda.	Interest	C.P.I.
1957	12	3	17	9	46	14	20	12	6	139	3.78	22.50
1958	20	6	26	23	63	14	20	13	7	192	2.29	23.10
1959	22	6	28	25	78	15	24	16	6	219	4.81	23.40
1960	20	6	26	24	70	13	22	15	6	202	3.32	23.70
1961	21	5	26	24	73	13	23	14	6	206	2.83	23.90
1962	24	7	29	26	69	14	23	12		203	4.01	24.20
1963	24	7	31	27	65	13	22	7		197	3.57	24.60
1964	27	8	38	33	96	19	22	1		244	3.74	25.10
1965	35	10	44	40	133	27	29			318	3.97	25.70
1966	39	11	48	44	151	31	31			355	5.00	26.60
1967	66	14	75	64	269	40	25			552	4.59	27.60
1968	73	16	84	72	387	49	26			708	6.25	28.70
1969	96	20	97	88	431	53	66			849	7.15	30.00
1970	97	20	100	93	420	55	99			884	6.12	31.00
1971	105	20	108	93	453	72	89			940	3.62	31.90
1972	114	25	124	103	534	68	102			1,070	3.55	33.40

Appendix Table 2 (continued)

Year	Nfld.	P.E.I.	N.S.	N.B.	Que.	Man.	Sask.	Alta.	B.C.	Cda.	Interest	C.P.I.
1973	156	33	186	146	737	113	116			1,487	5.39	36.00
1974	175	43	232	169	918	125	51			1,711	7.78	39.90
1975	189	48	252	187	1,049	151				1,877	7.37	44.20
1976	229	54	298	232	1,063	153	10			2,041	8.89	47.50
1977	278	63	342	273	1,322	237	58			2,573	7.35	51.30
1978	321	72	375	331	1,483	292	33			2,907	8.58	55.90
1979	344	81	428	310	1,766	344	74			3,346	11.57	61.00
1980	364	92	469	370	2,035	368	30			3,727	12.68	67.20
1981	427	107	528	445	2,490	399				4,395	17.78	75.50
1982	464	118	574	488	2,782	439				4,865	13.83	83.70
1983	540	125	605	517	2,977	466				5,229	9.32	88.50
1984	578	129	620	541	3,074	480				5,422	11.10	92.40
1985	653	134	596	604	2,728	427				5,143	9.46	96.00
1986	678	138	620	643	2,942	471	285			5,775	8.99	100.00
1987	807	163	734	724	3,151	727	299			6,605	8.17	104.40
1988	839	177	835	771	3,393	795	457			7,267	9.42	108.60

Appendix Table 2 (continued)

Year	Nfld.	P.E.I.	N.S.	N.B.	Que.	Man.	Sask.	Alta.	B.C.	Cda.	Interest	C.P.I.
1989	895	192	885	884	3,355	958	639			7,808	12.02	114.00
1990	919	194	949	868	3,627	915	531			8,002	12.81	119.50
1991	875	187	852	968	3,478	851	481			7,691	8.83	126.20
1992	879	167	864	851	3,647	836	483			7,727	6.51	128.10
1993	904	170	869	879	3,768	867	523			7,980	4.93	130.40
1994	960	186	931	923	3,865	964	687			8,516	5.42	130.7
SUM ($1994)	21,545	4,778	23,593	21,063	97,521	18,350	8,898	499	174	196,421		
PV ($1994)	35,730	8,072	40,048	35,045	164,687	29,854	13,921	11,101	390	328,848		

Source: *The Equalization Program*, Federal-Provincial Relations Division, Department of Finance, April 1994.

SUM is the combined value of the sum of all payments in 1994 dollars.
PV is the increment to the accumulated debts of the Provinces in 1994 if there had been no equalization payments, if the Provinces had borrowed what they received in equalization payments and if interest paid on the additional provincial borrowing were at the rate on 90-day Treasury bills of the federal government.
Interest is the average interest paid each year on 90-day Treasury Bills.
CPI is the Consumer Price Index set at 100 in 1986.